Tamyra Horst

Ratty Bathrobes, Cranky Kids, and Other Romantic Moments

Moving Your Marriage From Simmer to Sizzle

REVIEW AND HERALD® PUBLISHING ASSOCIATION
HAGERSTOWN, MD 21740

This book was
Edited by Penny Estes Wheeler
Copyedited by James Cavil
Designed by Toya Koch
Cover by Emily Harding
Typeset: 11/14 Usherwood Book

PRINTED IN U.S.A.

05 04 03 02 01   5 4 3 2 1

R&H Cataloging Service
Horst, Tamyra Lynn, 1961-
Ratty bathrobes, cranky kids, and other romantic moments
1. Marriage.I. Title.
646.78

ISBN 0-8280-1528-7

DEDICATION

To the ladies of the Mothers' Group—

Tanya, Kathy, Stacy, Wendy, Tina,

Minda, Lisa, Kristin, Deb, Karen—

who tirelessly chase after children,

love their husbands completely,

and have a passion for the Lord.

May He bless you with children

who always serve Him,

husbands who always love you,

and a relationship with Him

so close you can't describe it!

Other books by this author:
The Gift of Friendship (Pacific Press)
A Woman of Worth (Pacific Press)
How to Hug a Heart (Pacific Press)

To order, call 1-800-765-6955.
Visit our Web site at www.reviewandherald.com for information on other Review and Herald products.

CONTENTS

CHAPTER 1

Where Did the Romance Go?

I have rarely seen couples so openly adore each other. The way he looked into her eyes and bragged about her. The way they held hands everywhere they went. Sometimes when they were looking at each other I had to wonder, *Do they even realize anyone else is in this room?* I don't remember their names, but I met them while standing in line for a meal at a conference at which I was speaking. I watched them all weekend and loved every moment of it. Whether attending seminars together, strolling in the moonlight to the evening activities, they were always holding hands. It made me miss Tim. Seeing them so obviously in love caused me to long to be with my husband. I wanted to hike with him around the beautiful lake I could see through my bedroom window. I wanted to snuggle with him by the fireplace in the lobby.

As I thought about Tim, I began to wonder, *Where has our romance gone? Do we still gaze deeply into each other's eyes and find our-*

selves alone in a roomful of people? When we talk about one another, is it to brag as proudly as this husband did of his wife, with a love so obvious that it was written all over his face?

Tim and I love each other, but life has become so busy. Is there still room for romance in our lives? Is there room for romance in yours?

Is romance limited to the young? to the newly married and yet-to-be married couples? The couple I watched all weekend had been married for a long time. They'd raised a family together. Do you have time for romance only when the children are grown and gone?

Today all we know is busyness. Everyone is rushing somewhere. So much to do. Our to-do list is longer than the hours we're awake. We feel guilty when we don't accomplish all the things we think we should. Work. Family. Church. Exercise. Time with God. Eating healthful meals. Finding time to prepare healthful meals. Our children have music lessons, karate lessons, baseball games. We fall into bed at the end of the day, exhausted, lying next to an equally exhausted spouse. Glancing at each other through half closed eyes, we wonder if we'll ever have time for romance again. Will we ever have a whole moment of quiet just for us? Can we ever look deeply into each other's eyes without falling asleep?

We watch newlyweds in church. Holding hands and sitting shoulder against shoulder. The scent of freesia and roses surround her. He holds the door for her. She laughs at his jokes. We hear them talk of the things they've been up to. Going out for a quiet dinner. Walking through the swirling autumn leaves on a warm fall afternoon. She's planning a weekend getaway at a little bed and breakfast in the mountains to celebrate their sixth anniversary—

sixth-*month* anniversary. He brings her flowers and compliments her cooking. And we wonder, *Was there really a time when we were like that?*

Where did the romance go? And more important, can we ever get it back?

I remember when Tanya and I first became friends. They'd just moved to our area, and I was jealous. She and her husband were newly married, and he was her biggest fan. Always praising her. Complimenting her, and not just to her, but to other people. At prayer meeting. At church. It seemed as though he was *always* saying something nice about her. He sent her roses. Took her out to dinner. She spent almost all of her free time with him.

There'd been a time when Tim and I were constantly together. We worked at the same office, so we drove to and from work together. Passed each other in the halls. Ate lunch together. At church we served on the same committees. Sat in the same Sabbath school classes. We spent lazy Sabbath afternoons walking at parks. We went grocery shopping together. Ate out. Stayed up late on Saturday nights eating pizza and watching old movies. Walked hand in hand at the mall.

Then we had a baby.

All of a sudden Tim was heading off to work and I was wondering if I'd possibly have time to take a shower and fix dinner before he came home. Sleepless nights and two crying babies took their toll. Sleep became a precious, rare commodity. Most days I felt as if I was feeling my way through a fog. Romance was the last thing on my mind. Sex often felt like another responsibility, another demand, rather than something I looked forward to and enjoyed. I just wanted to be able to go to sleep. And I didn't feel sexy. Most days I felt frumpy and unattractive. I understood why candlelight was the preferred lighting for women.

A few years passed, and the boys grew older. I got a full night's sleep and felt human again. But life doesn't usually get easier. Just different. Different challenges. It's the same with romance. Now that the reasons for my lack of feeling romantic were gone, you'd think life would go back to that newlywed bliss. But guess what—it didn't!

Every day is full of new demands. Deadlines. Things to do. Errands to run. Phone calls. Meetings to attend. It never seems to end.

A normal day in our household begins between 5:00 and 5:30. By 7:00 I've tried to have a meaningful quiet devotional time, I've walked or jogged a mile, packed lunches, set breakfast things out, taken a shower, and finally woke everyone else up. By 7:30 Tim is out the door. The boys and I quickly follow and head to school—the opposite direction of Tim's office. The day passes in a blur as I check things off of a full to-do list. Attempting to do not only the urgent but the important. Then it's time to pick up the boys from school, fix dinner, supervise their homework, and get ready for bed and another day. By the time the boys are in bed, I'm ready to head there myself. But that's usually the first quiet moment Tim and I have had together all day. The only time to talk. To snuggle. To enjoy each other's company.

Romance or sleep? That's a tough choice some nights. There are times that I'd really rather go to sleep. I have mornings like that too. When I'd rather sleep than get up for my quiet time with my Father. But in both cases I've made a commitment to a relationship. And I know that it means sacrifice, investing both time and energy. Romance isn't something that just happens. It requires planning and time.

Is it worth it? Why should you bother putting the energy

into adding romance to your marriage?

ROMANCE MAKES YOUR RELATIONSHIP STRONG. Romance bonds us together. As we rush around with so much to do, it's easy for couples to drift apart. To be so busy that when things finally slow down and husband and wife find themselves in a quiet house—just the two of them—they have nothing to talk about. They don't know what's happening in each other's lives. They don't share anything in common. Without putting the effort into a relationship, it's easy to drift apart. In fact, it's inevitable.

"When John and I got married, I never thought much about romance. It seemed silly. We worked long days, and there was a house to clean, children to raise, bills to pay," says Emily, who has been married for 43 years. "Then one day the kids were all gone. John and I found ourselves sitting across from each other at the supper table, and I didn't know what to say to him. I looked at this man, whom I love fiercely, and wondered what to talk about. What was he interested in? Everything in our lives had always revolved around the children. Now that they were gone, *who were we?*"

Kelly doesn't know what she'd do without her "dates" with her husband. "Wayne and I have a baby-sitter who knows that we need her the third weekend every month. Sometimes we go out to eat. Sometimes we just go somewhere to walk. It's a time for us to talk. Really talk. Not about the bills or the kids, but about each other. About what's on our minds and hearts. I look forward to these weekends. I count the days till the next date. Sometimes it helps me through the week, knowing that I have a date coming up."

"I thought Katie was a little crazy to suggest that we go

on regular dates. We're married, and I thought the dating was over," Brian told me. He and Katie have been married for seven years. "But I said OK, whatever. And it's surprised me how much I look forward to the dates. It's a time for me to have Katie's attention all to myself. No interruptions. No phone calls. Nothing. Just her and me. We can really talk about stuff. I've realized that I need this time together as much as she does."

ROMANCE MODELS MARRIAGE FOR OUR CHILDREN. "Isn't it time for you and Dad to go on another date, Mom?" Zachary asked me one afternoon as we drove home from school. I knew why he was asking. It wasn't because he realized how important it was for Tim and me to spend time together, just the two of us. Or because he wanted us to have special time together. He just wanted to go play at his friend's house. Junior's mom and I trade baby-sitting once a month so we each can have a night out with our husbands without baby-sitting costs for either of us. Sometimes we get busy and put off our date night, but before long one of the kids is urging us to go out so they can play with their friends.

Even though Zack didn't understand how important it is for Tim and me to spend time together and grow closer to each other, he's seeing that it is important to *us*. He's seeing us make it a priority in our lives. Whether it's an evening out while he and his brother are at a friend's or their grandmom's, or a day together while they're in school, Zack and Josh are watching and learning about marriage. They're learning from us. We're their example. What they learn from Tim and me will impact their relationships with girls and their marriages.

Just think how lucky your child's spouse will be to have

a husband or wife who, throughout childhood, watched his parents date and snuggle and maintain a close relationship with each other. What a difference it will make to their marriages and their families.

"I remember watching Mom and Dad," Autumn says with a smile. "After dinner Dad would assign kitchen duty to each of us and he'd take Mom out on the porch. In the summer they'd sit on the porch swing with a glass of lemonade and swing and talk for about an hour. In the winter they'd head for the family room with mugs of hot chocolate or tea. No kids were allowed. We knew not to interrupt—or to fight with each other and cause them to come check on us. This was Mom and Dad's time together. I loved to peek in and see Dad with his arm around Mom. I knew that kind of love was what I wanted when I grew up."

IT GIVES OUR CHILDREN A SENSE OF SECURITY. "You know, Mom," Joshua said to me as we drove home from school one afternoon, "most of the kids in my class have two dads." (It's amazing the things we talk about in the car on the way to and from school.) Josh attended a small one-room conservative Christian school. And all but three or four families were headed by single parents or parents who were remarried. Most of the students either had no dad in the home, or two dads—one at home and one somewhere else.

I felt that there was more to Josh's statement than what he was saying. "Does that make you worry sometimes that it could happen to our family? That Dad and I could split up?"

"Yeah, I guess."

It's a common fear among today's children. Whether it's spoken or goes unsaid, most of them notice that the parents of their friends are splitting up. They may not know the statistics, but they know it's happening. And it's natural for them to worry.

But when Mom and Dad are spending time together, snuggling, talking, holding hands, it helps kids feel more secure. When they can see and feel the love between their parents, they intuitively know that they're committed to each other. When you *make* the time to be alone with your husband or wife, you are modeling love to your kids.

When Tim comes home after a day at work, we greet each other with hugs and kisses. Often the boys are there in the kitchen when Tim arrives. They groan and grin when they see us kissing, but I know they love it. They like knowing that Dad enjoys being with Mom. That he can't wait to get home to her. It gives them a reason to believe that they're not going to have two dads. And kids want their mom and dad to stay together.

IT'S GOOD FOR US. Romance reminds us that someone loves us. That someone cares. It makes us smile.

"I like the little notes Barb tucks in my lunch occasionally," shares John. "It reminds me that she loves me. That she must think I'm special."

"At the end of the day, when it's just Tom and I, I breathe a sigh of relief," Sally says with a sigh. My job is so stressful. Everyone at work needs something from me constantly. Then I come home to a ton of other things that need to be done. But when Tom and I finally sit down together . . . " Sally pauses; her face shines. "Well, at last I can relax. I can tell Tom about my day and know that he cares. Sometimes he'll rub my shoulders or my feet. It's the best part of my day."

IT MAKES MEMORIES. I can still visualize the rhododendron-lined pathway. The bright, clear sun making the afternoon almost hot. Tim had taken the day off to spend with me before the boys were out of school for the summer. We spent most of the day hiking in a park. Small memories flit across my mind like butterflies. They might be insignificant to anyone else, but for me they just sing! Eating hoagies from a newly opened shop while we watched swans gliding across a small pond. The tiny Chinese restaurant near town—the first Chinese food we'd ever eaten. Walking at "Roots' Market," inhaling the rich vegetable scents, the sharp, sweet fragrances of fruit. Buying produce.

Then I think of the bubble bath Tim ran for me just the other day. Our upstairs isn't finished yet; the walls are still studs. The upstairs doesn't even have running water yet. How did I manage a bubble bath? Tim made trip after trip up and down the stairs with buckets of hot water until my brand-new tub was filled with plumeria-scented bubbles. (You'll understand why this is so important when I tell you that we'd had only showers for the previous 13 years.) He brought up a compact disc player and put on a favorite piano CD. And I had no clue what he was up to. I was busy putting the boys to bed and studying the lesson I was going to teach that weekend. When Tim asked if I wanted to take a bath, I wasn't sure what he was talking about. But lying there in that sweet, fragrant water was almost heaven.

(As I'm writing this, Tim and his father are finishing the upstairs plumbing. Just a minute ago Tim came to kiss me again—he takes a break often when he passes the computer—and asked if I'd like another bath tonight. And of course I told him I did. Even if this time the water will rush through the tub faucet instead of being hauled upstairs in buckets by my loving, creative husband.)

Those down times when marriage gets tough—and it does—memories of the sweet things you've done for each other keep you going. You have days—or weeks—when you wonder if you're still in love. When he's made you so angry, you could just scream. Or she's been so busy that you wonder if she even remembers your name. This is the time to remember the good times, the sweet, thoughtful times you've shared. You'll be reminded that you *do* love each other. That the tough moments pass. That you really enjoy being together. It makes you want to patch things up and make another memory.

Life is busy. Sometimes we forget to take the time for the little things, like romance. The little extras that say "I love you!" But it's important. Romance makes your marriage stronger. It gives you memories to hang on to. And teaches your kids what love can be like, giving them security and ideas for when they're married. Romance is more than lace and candles and warm, fuzzy feelings. It's a source of strength and security. It's an investment in your future—the future of your relationship.

It's an important part of your marriage, yours and mine.

CHAPTER 2

Dating Again?

R emember your first date? You took twice as long as usual in the bathroom, working with your hair, getting everything just perfect—while your siblings pounded on the door. Your bedroom floor was puddled with outfits that you tried on but weren't quite right. Your heart flip-flopped and your stomach was full of butterflies as you and a nervous fellow teen rode off together in a parent's station wagon.

I had my first date with a guy from work, double dating with my brother and his girlfriend. The four of us spent the afternoon at a park, where we rented a rowboat and played on the lake. The guys broke the oarlocks on the boat while rowing too deeply. And once we were home, I fell off his front porch when he tried kissing me goodbye. (We actually did go out again.)

We often think that dating is reserved for couples who aren't married. It's a way for them to get to know each other. An opportunity to have fun. And sometimes the purpose of dating is to get to know a guy or girl before marrying them.

But once you're married, dating ends. Doesn't it?

While the boys were still young, Tim and I made a commitment to "date" once a month. We realized how easy it was for us to get so busy that we didn't have time for just the two of us, and we didn't want our relationship to coast away. We were willing to put the time and effort into making and keeping our marriage fun and close. So we promised ourselves time. Dates.

At times it's been tough. And we've missed a month. Or two. Or three. But the commitment is there. And *commitment* is the word. We're committed to our relationship; our dates aren't something we require of each other. It's far more than that. We want to be friends as well as wife and husband. To remain friends. Always. I want to be a support and encouragement to Tim. I want him to know that he always has at least one person on his side, supporting him, cheering him on. And I need to know that he loves me. No matter what. Our dates and the little things we do for each other give us tangible expressions of our love for each other. It's our love in action. And sometimes the action increases our love.

But once you've made the decision to add more romance to your lives—to date, to spend time together—there's just one little thing. What's a date? It might be so long since you've had one that you don't know anymore. Where do you begin?

A while back I found a picture in a magazine that I just loved. It was so *real!* A guy and girl were sitting in a rowboat in the middle of a lake on a lazy, sunny afternoon. The water was quiet, and no one else was around. The photo's caption said it all: *She's lost in the wonder of romance. He wonders if the fish are biting.*

ROMANCE IS DIFFERENT TO MEN AND WOMEN. Men define romance in a more physical way than women do. Lingerie. Steamy nights. Mystery and passion. One survey showed that 95 percent of men thought of sex when they thought of romance. Only 5 percent of women described romance the same way. The first time I went to a church to speak on romance and marriage, Tim was shocked. "You're going to talk about *what?*"

Women love to be courted. Flowers. Candlelight. Holding hands. Snuggling—with no other expectations. Women tend to love the details of the moment. Music. Atmosphere. And we love for our husbands to take care of the details, to plan it all. We often look at the message behind the moment. And behind the gifts.

I'll never forget one birthday when Tim gave me a gift from the ultrafeminine, ultrasexy woman's store, Victoria's Secret. It was in a big box, and when Tim handed the box to me he said, "When I saw this I thought of you."

I couldn't wait to get it opened. I was excited that he'd thought of me, that he'd gone into this store to find something just for me—something pretty, feminine, and sexy. Isn't that what he thought of me? But the garment I pulled out was not pretty, nor feminine, nor sexy. He'd said that he thought of me when he'd seen it. *Just what had he thought?* The garment was cotton, not silk. It was cut like an A, and it reminded me of something Ma would have worn on the old TV series *Little House on the Prairie.* I was puzzled, and I didn't feel complimented. Tim said that he thought it looked so comfortable, he just knew I'd enjoy it. But I was hoping for something pretty and lacy.

Men don't often think about the message that women

will read into their gifts. Usually men think practical. (And most men have long ago given up on trying to figure out what women think.) My friend Ann's husband gave her a central vacuum system for Mother's Day. (Actually, it was something she wanted and was thrilled to receive. But it makes my point.) Tim is the number one practical gift giver. He loves to give me coats. To keep me warm. His way of taking care of me. Of saying "I love you." He's given me pots and pans. Flannel pajamas. A rowing machine. (I did need to trim down after having a baby.) I used to be disappointed in his choices, for I longed for gifts that spoke of love and romance. Pretty things. Personal things. But I've learned that his gifts do speak of love, *his* way of loving me. *His* way of saying "You're special to me, and I'm always going to take care of you." And sometimes his gifts are not only practical, they're incredibly sweet. This past Christmas I couldn't figure out why he gave me an empty basket. It was a nice basket, but it was just a basket. "You need a new worship basket," Tim explained. "This one's nice and sturdy. I think everything will fit in it." I was very touched by his thoughtfulness. I didn't know he'd even noticed how beat-up the second-hand basket where I kept my Bible, journal, and other things I used for my personal worship had become.

Men and women do have different ways of showing love. Of thinking about romance. Of saying "I care. I think you're special." I might say "I love you" by putting a little card in Tim's lunch, building a snowman in the front yard with the kids and putting a "Welcome home, Dad" sign on it, or by offering a back rub on a stressful day. Tim has said "I love you" by changing the oil in my car before I drove to a retreat or, most recently, putting new tires on my car before I drove several hours to a seminar. I show my love through little kindnesses, words, and gifts. He shows his love by taking care of me.

We have different ideas of what a fun date is, too. When Tim plans a date, we're more likely to hike or bike. For one anniversary he suggested par four golfing. Another time he took me to a driving range. For me, a romantic date includes holding hands, walking on a misty beach, sitting in front of a blazing fire, and eating by candlelight. Dates I've planned have included take-out Chinese food by the fireplace with soft music in the background, and a candlelight retreat in the attic while rain splattered on the roof. (Our attic was one with a roof high enough to walk under.)

But despite our differences, we agree that we want to spend time together, for we want to make our marriage stronger. We want to know each other and love each other. We don't want busyness or the stress of life to come between us. Romance and dating are details that can make our lives fuller and closer.

What are the ingredients of a good date?

LAUGHTER. Life is serious. Bills. Work. Problems. The news. So much to think about. To take care of. Too little laughter. Laughing together isn't just fun; it draws us closer. And it's good for us. How long has it been since you've *really* laughed? Or you and your spouse have laughed together?

Recently, a friend and I planned a surprise fortieth birthday party for friends—a grown-ups-only party. One friend planned several games, and Tina and I decorated. I couldn't wait till the big night! Why? Because I knew we would be laughing. I knew that it would be fun. I couldn't wait to laugh. And we did laugh. We laughed so hard that even many of the guys had tears streaming down their faces. I remember looking at Tim at one point during one of the games and saw him laughing. I thought, *I don't remember seeing him like that in a long time. I can't ever remember when I've seen him laugh like that.*

He'd been working hard on our house for months. The week before Christmas, friends came over and helped him take off the entire roof and attic. When they left, our house was flat and the steps that led up into the attic climbed into the night sky. By January we had a second story on our home. But that was just been the beginning. Walls needed studded out. Electric wiring put in. Plumbing hooked up. Insulation. Phone and cable TV lines. Heating. Drywall. Floors. An overwhelming task. On top of all that, there was his daytime work which is always stressful. And church.

Beyond that, Tim had a major conflict in his life with another person whom he couldn't avoid. He'd been working constantly, with little time to laugh. I loved seeing him laugh the way he did that evening! (So many people enjoyed the evening and the laughter, that we've decided we need to do it more often, even if no one is turning 40. We need fun and laughter in our lives.)

Playing games or telling funny stories and jokes can make you laugh. Check out a joke book from the library and learn a few new ones that you know you'll both enjoy. Play a funny practical joke on your spouse. Read a humor book together. Have a tickle battle. Do something silly together. Go to the park and play on the swings and see-saw—without the kids. Smile. Giggle. Laugh.

ENCOURAGEMENT. All of us need encouragement, but where does that encouragement come from? Your boss? Not too often. People you run into during the day? Probably not. If you want your spouse to be encouraged, you're the best source for it. And a date is a great place to start. Tell your husband what you like about him. Tell your wife what you appreciate about her. Little things. Big things. Maybe it's been so long since you paid a compliment that you have to stop and think about it a while. It will be a grand investment of your time.

Let him know that he did a great job with the latest house project. Tell her that she's a great mom. Thank him for working or for spending time with the kids. Let her know that you'd be lost without her. If you don't encourage your spouse, letting him know that you believe in him, telling her that she can do it and does a great job at it, who will?

TIME. Time is such a precious commodity. All of us could use a little more of it. You may not feel that you have time to date, but you'll always find time to do the things that are most important to you. You and I need to realize how important the little things are in our relationships and make time to make them a priority. It doesn't have to be huge chunks of time. Even little bits of time helps. A few minutes to snuggle. A quick walk around the block. A couple hours to go out for dinner. But a day or a weekend together will provide memories and fun to last over the busy and sometimes rough times to come.

Tim occasionally takes a day off to spend with me while the boys are at school. I clear my schedule. (Working from my home gives me a lot of flexibility.) We drop the boys at school and head out. Sometimes our time together includes things that have to be done. Just this week Tim took a day off to get tires on my car and pick up some things for the house. (He's getting ready to put the siding on.) We did the chores together. First we went out for breakfast, giving us a brief moment to sit and talk. Then we headed to the garage and the home building supply warehouse. We spent more than three hours in two different building supply places. Not my idea of romance, but hey! We even disagreed a little on some odds and ends. But then we met in the tool section, and we both apologized and kissed. That was a little romantic. Well, maybe not romantic, but I liked it. We held hands as we walked back to pick up the car.

Most of the time we give each other is short. An evening together. An hour after the boys are in bed. A walk around the block in the early morning of the weekends. But sometimes we can spend a day together. To hike. Or go "touristing" in the little shops near us. And once or twice in our marriage we've managed a few days away. Just us.

Time is an important commodity. Invest some of it in your marriage. You'll never regret it. Remember that a date doesn't have to take hours or a whole day. It can be just moments. Romance happens when you step away from everything else and focus on each other. Romance involves being together, reconnecting with each other.

Sneak in time. Kiss in the morning. Tuck a love note in his lunch or pocket as he heads for work. Write a little note and leaved it taped to the mirror where she'll find it. Make heart-shaped biscuits or pancakes. Whisper suggestive nothings in his ear as you hug him goodbye. Or hello. Do chores together—adding laughter, jokes, hand holding, touching, eye contact, encouraging words. Meet for lunch. Hold hands in church. Go for a walk around the block after supper. Or before breakfast. I love to walk in the mornings, and that's usually when I exercise. Tim doesn't join me during the week, but often on weekends he'll get up and walk with me.

Taking time with your spouse will be one of the most

important investments you'll ever make in your marriage.

Laughter. Encouragement. Time. These are the beginnings of a great date. Your time together with your mate will strengthen your marriage—and you. You'll enjoy life more as you enjoy each other, and thereby feel even more loved. It's a gift you can give your spouse and your marriage, and you'll end up getting back much more than you've given.

WHO DOES THE ASKING? "Sometimes I just want George to plan the date," Laura sighs. "I'd love for him to bring me flowers or candy. To call me from work and say, 'Hey, honey, don't make dinner tonight. I'm bringing something home.' Or to ask me out. That might not ever happen, and might seem silly to him, but I'd love for him to call me at work and ask me out." She giggles. "That would be so much fun. It would make me feel young again."

Most women would love for their husbands to ask them out. To plan a date. To bring home flowers—or send them. To bring home candy or a gift for no reason at all. And some husbands *are* romantic. Jan's husband has planned a surprise anniversary trip. She has no idea where they're going. He's told her that he'll give her two hours' notice and then they're headed out of the country. (She thinks maybe Mexico.) Pam just got back from a trip Kerry had planned. He told her what kind of clothes to pack, but she had no clue where they were going until she stood at the ticket counter and got her boarding pass.

But it's probably fair to say that most times it's the wives who end up responsible for planning time together—if it's going to happen. And while we'd love our husbands to take the initiative, we have to ask ourselves, "What's more important? That we have time together or that he plans it?"

Usually it's more important to have the time together.

But for those occasions that it's very important for him to take the initiative, *tell him.* Get his attention first, but don't plant yourself between him and a playoff game. That won't work! Instead, tell him, "I need time with you, but I need for you to be the one to plan it. When you take the time to plan a special time with me, it makes me know that you think it's important too." Then tell him why it's important to you.

Tim's been so busy and so distracted lately—working on the house, taking care of other things—that I've felt a little neglected. I've tried to spend time with him while he's working on the house, but it's not enough. I need for him to want to spend time with me. So I told him. I let him know that I need to have time with him when he could focus only on me—not on the siding, the computer monitor, or anything else. After all, he doesn't know what I'm thinking or feeling until I tell him.

When your husband or wife does plan something, let them know how much you appreciate it. Say thank you. Tell him that it made you feel loved and cared about. Send her an e-mail and let her know what you enjoyed most. With a little encouragement, it might just happen again.

CHAPTER 3

Romance Killers

The setting was perfect. A warm fire glowed in the fireplace, and soft music played on the stereo. Two glasses of chilled nonalcoholic bubbly sat on the table beside a plate of artistically arranged fruit and cheese. The children were tucked into bed. It was just Jim and Karen. Alone. Karen had planned every detail of the evening, even to splashing on the perfume Jim loved. They had so little time together, just the two of them. The next hours would be special.

Karen breathed deeply as they sat down to this perfect evening. She was going to enjoy every minute of it. She'd waited a long time for this.

Then the phone rang. "Let the answering machine get it," she called as Jim jumped up. But he answered it anyway, and returned 20 minutes later. The fire had died down. The bubbly was warm, and Karen was cold. She abruptly got up and headed for bed.

"Where are you going?" Jim called after her as the door slammed. "What's wrong?"

ROMANCE KILLERS. They're all around you. Small things and big things that threaten to take the sparkle out of your time together. What are they, and what can you do about them?

STRESS. Stress is one of the big romance killers, and we live with it every day. The sources of stress in our lives— yours and mine—are too numerous to list. Bills. Finances. Taxes. Who does what housework? For some of us, work is stressful. You may have stressful relationships in your life. Parents. In-laws. Coworkers. Traffic. Projects around the house. All the demands you put on yourself, that others put on you, or things you think others put on you. If you've had a stressful day at the office it may be hard to unwind for a fun evening out, especially if the topic of conversation over dinner is work. Regardless of the source, stress wears you out *and* can literally make you sick. Then to make matters worse, in the middle of everything that's pulling at you and pushing you down, you attempt to spend special time with your spouse? *Help!*

Romance and stress just don't go together.

What can you do?

First, don't let stress enter your special time together. Guard that time. At the end of an especially difficult day, do something that helps relieve your stress. Soak in a hot bubble bath. (I like mine with candlelight and music.) Ask your husband for a massage. Go for a fast-paced walk (or a slow stroll). Listen to uplifting or soothing music on the way home from work. Take a few moments before your date to sit quietly and relax. Unwind. De-stress.

Set aside other time to talk about the things that cause stress in your life. Don't go out for a nice dinner together and rehash the problems at work, or the trouble the kids are having at school, or how the bills are going to be paid. Talk about these things beforehand. If you're going out on Wednesday night, set aside time on Tuesday night to talk about the things that are bugging you. If certain topics are always stressful, ban them from date night conversations.

Sometimes Tim's job is stressful; sometimes it's not. I like for him to talk to me about work. I enjoy knowing what's going on with him while he's gone all day. So I appreciate his sharing with me what he's working on at the office. But when work is stressful—when things aren't going well and it's a source of irritation for him—I don't want to talk about it during our date time. It ruins the mood. It's hard for him to enjoy the evening when he's still focusing on work.

So we talk about work before we go out. Or afterward, if he can put it out of his thoughts. The point is to ban stressful topics from your date.

TOPICS OF CONVERSATION. And that leads us to the next romance killer—topics of conversation. What you talk about when you're together will definitely affect your date, for better or for worse. We've already banned stress-related topics, but other romance-killing issues can sneak into your conversations too.

This isn't the place to complain about the kids—or anyone else, for that matter. It's not time to list all the things that need to be done around the house. Remember that sitting down to a romantic dinner at the Olive Garden is not the time to drag out your honey-do list. Or to remind your spouse that she needs to get back to her exercise program.

(Another chapter will discuss what to talk about on your dates, including suggestions for meaningful conversation.) Complaining or nagging are definitely not romantic.

INTERRUPTIONS. He's staring deeply into her eyes. She smiles coyly as she tilts her head ever so slightly toward him. Their lips gently touch; their bodies ease closer together. Then the phone rings.

Phone calls in the middle of a date can put an end to romance. And with cell phones, your phone calls can follow you anywhere. I was out to dinner just the other day and saw a couple sitting together, but they weren't talking to each other. She was on the phone.

Let the answering machine pick up the call. If it's an emergency, you can take it right there, and if not, they'll call back. We've made a family rule that we don't answer the phone during dinner, family worship, most visits with friends, or time with just Tim and me. Sometimes one of us breaks the rule, but for the most part we just let the machine pick up. It's a matter of deciding what's most important at that moment. For us, family time is more important than phone calls.

Remove the computer, the TV, and video games from the bedroom. These can be such a distraction or temptation. Sometimes watching a movie together while snuggled in bed will make for a fun date. But too often having a TV in the bedroom gives the opportunity to channel-surf instead of talk. And watching movies may be a relaxing date, but it's not one that builds your relationship. Sure, you're spending time together, but usually not with a lot of communication. So while it may be fun once in a while, it shouldn't be the main event. Not if you want the opportunity to talk and to continue learning more about each other.

Many of our dates have been in the evening after the kids are in bed. It's saved finding a baby-sitter, and when they were younger their bedtime was fairly early, so we had a whole evening together. But if your kids are home and in bed, make sure they're asleep before you start your date. Little ones seem to have a sense of when grown-ups want quiet time and often "need" things. A drink of water. A story. Another trip to the pottie. If your children are older, tell them they're not to come into the living room, bedroom, back porch—wherever you are—unless it's a matter of life or death. Let them know that this is time for the two of you. It will take a while before they understand how important this is to you, but they'll learn. Our boys often lie in their room and talk for a while, and that's OK with us. But after they're in bed, it's our time.

More than anything else, errands have interrupted our dates. Trips to the hardware store or home building supply warehouse. Not very romantic. Sometimes it's necessary, or at least it seems to be, but don't make the mistake of restricting your dates to errands and other things that have to be done. Tuck in some time for fun. Stop off for ice cream. Drive the long way home and stop and watch the ducks in a park. Don't let dates be nothing more than both of you doing chores together. Sometimes doing chores and errands will suffice as a date—but only if you learn to make it fun.

YOUR THOUGHTS: ANOTHER ROMANCE KILLER. Your thoughts can be one of the biggest romance killers of them all. *My* thoughts are usually racing a mile a minute, with several projects tumbling around my mind at once. Grocery lists. Things to do. Errands to run. People to call. Replaying conversations. Remembering things I need to tell or to ask others. By the time the day ends I'm already planning tomorrow.

Most of the time, romance just isn't a part of our thoughts. Sometimes even when we're alone together, attempting to have fun together, our thoughts are somewhere else. Mine have been. Tim and I are snuggling, or walking hand in hand (he knows I love to go walking), and he's talking—telling me nice things about me or what he's been thinking we could do together—and I'm trying to remember if I told Carol that the meeting was going to be on Wednesday night instead of Tuesday. Have you been there?

How do you control those thoughts? How do you prepare your mind for that romantic interlude?

During the day, before your time together, think about your husband. What do you like about him? What characteristics do you admire? Think about how he looks. Focus on those features you love. That twinkle in his eyes. His strong arms. What are the little things he's done that makes you smile?

Think about your spouse while you clean. Or make copies at the copier. Or fill another order. Whenever you're doing something and can let your thoughts wander, let them wander to her.

Plan out a romantic date in your mind. Where would you go? What would you do? Replay the dates you've enjoyed.

Let your spouse know you're thinking about him. I often e-mail Tim at work, just to say that I'm thinking of him. I share a couple thoughts. I know it makes him smile and quite possibly makes him more eager to come home to me. Occasionally I'll call him at work. And once in a while he's called me. These calls aren't about "important" things. It's just to let the other know that you're thinking of them. It's often the highlight of our day. Sometimes I've smiled all afternoon every time I thought of Tim's call.

Taking the time to prepare yourself for the date, doing those little extra things, can turn your thoughts to romance. Make the effort to do things that make you feel prettier, such as putting on perfume or scented body lotion. Try out a new hairstyle. Choose an outfit that makes you feel good, that you know he likes. Terri loves to wear colorful underwear under her clothes. It makes her feel more feminine. For Tracy, it's taking the time to do her nails (something she never does as often as she'd like), for it makes her feel well groomed. Sometimes I smooth on a certain lotion Tim bought for me at Victoria's Secret. It has sparkles in it, and I especially like it in the summer when the sun reflects on a thousand sparkles. It's softly scented, too.

What makes *you* feel more attractive? Take the time to do it. It'll help your mind to anticipate even more the time you'll be spending together.

Once you're on your date—whether it's going out or at home—attempt to keep your thoughts focused on the moment. When you find yourself mentally listing all the things you need to do when the evening is over, lean over and kiss your spouse. Remind yourself that this isn't the time to think about work. It's time to enjoy each other. Think about what you've planned for this date—or could plan still. Remember what you've been thinking about all day, or simply tell your husband that you love him.

SCHEDULE IT. Time, or the lack of it, is another romance killer. We just never have enough time for everything we want or need to do. The lack of time kills romance before it has a chance to start. How do you find time for a few minutes—or hours—of romantic time together?

Schedule it in. Just as you set aside time for a doctor's

appointment or a trip to the grocery store. Remind yourself that this is very important—for your relationship, for you, and for your children. Every moment you spend with your spouse having fun, enjoying each other, and communicating beyond the daily surface talk is an investment in your marriage. You and I always find time to do the things that are important to us. Make this something that's truly important to you.

Write it on the calendar. Plan ahead. Have regular date times. Remind your husband as you leave for work in the morning. Call your wife at the office or home and let her know that you can't wait. Don't let other things bump it from your calendar. Treat it as you do all other commitments. For that's what it is: a commitment to your marriage. To your spouse. A way of saying, "I love you, and our relationship is important to me."

Tim and I have often had a weekly date time. It's 10:00 on Thursday nights, and we watch a certain TV program together. And yes, we talk. Occasionally we eat popcorn, and we always snuggle. Sometimes he falls asleep. (Remember, TV and movies aren't the best dates.) But it's a weekly commitment, and no matter what he's working on, he stops and meets me at 10:00. If we're out, we try to be home. It's the one show we've made a point to watch.

As I write this, it's summer and time for reruns, so we're not stopping to watch TV. Instead I've been hanging around the construction process, watching him work, and helping out when I can. (Tonight, however, he's working on scaffolding outside the window while I type. Our oldest son is out there with him, so they're having father-son time.) But we've learned that we must make time to talk and keep up with each other's lives.

Another date we enjoy during the winter is talking over

a cup of tea. One night I even found crumpets and served them. (Tim loved them; I didn't.) At the end of the day, after the boys were tucked in and Tim had finished work for the evening, I put on a pot of water and pulled out a couple mugs. By the time the tea cooled and was drunk, we'd had time to talk and were ready to go to sleep.

Don't get bogged down in thinking that a date is always going out for dinner. It can be staying home. And it doesn't require a whole evening or day. It can last a few hours or a few moments. It's just stepping away from everything else and focusing on each other. Being together. Reconnecting with each other.

Make the time. It's one of the best investments you can make.

IT'S MONEY, HONEY. Money. Another romance killer. Or it can be. Sometimes we think that a date has to cost money. A baby-sitter. Dinner. Or any other activity that you decide to do. And for some of us, extra money is hard to come by. It's hard enough to get all the bills paid. But it's the same as with time—you and I find the money for the things that are most important to us.

Keep a jar to drop in your loose change at the end of the day (or the week). Each evening, empty your pockets or wallet into it. It's surprising how quickly it adds up. Make it a part of your budget. It doesn't have to be a huge part. Or simply set aside a dollar or two a week. You may be surprised that you hardly miss it. And before long you have enough for a treat for two.

Then, too, it's surprising the things you can do for free.

Instead of paying a baby-sitter, Tim and I, and many of our friends, simply find another couple who want a monthly date too, and switch off baby-sitting. One night a month we watch their kids, and one night a month they watch ours. We've had someone to switch with since the boys were little. And many times our dates have been after the boys were in bed.

Once you've found the time and have found someone to keep your kids, you'll discover all kinds of free things to do. Hiking at the county park; guided tours or classes. Some parks have free concerts in the summertime. And often local churches will offer free programs. In our area several museums are open one day a year without the usual fee. Tim and I have gone "touristing" together—our word for pretending to be tourists in our own area and visiting all the little shops. We've picnicked in a park, by a stream, or out in the backyard. We've laid a blanket in the backyard on warm August nights and watched for falling stars. We've walked around the mall or just sat and watched people—trying to decide what they might do for a living.

Take a moonlight stroll. Fill a room with candles and soft music. Sit by a fire (outside or inside). Go wading in a stream. Be creative.

What are the things that kill romance in your life? What are the reasons that you don't date? Or that your dates aren't fun? Look for ways to overcome these obstacles. Make your time together fun and special.

CHAPTER 4

Creating the Mood

I once read that romance is a combination of environment, emotions, and enjoyment, and that the environment can affect your emotions and enjoyment. But there's a positive aspect to this, for you can definitely build or create the environment in which you spend your special time together.

Kay lit the candles she'd placed throughout the room—all 50 of them—and the scent of vanilla slowly filled the air. Music softly played in the background. She looked in the mirror one more time. Phil would be home in only a couple more minutes. She smiled at her reflection, anticipating her husband's reaction to the long, flowing red robe she wore. Red was his favorite color.

Dorothy was amazed when Bob opened the door for her to enter the family room. He'd promised her some time together, just the two of them, and said that he'd take care of the details. And he had! As she scanned what had been an all-purpose room she saw a "beach." Bob had pushed the furniture against the walls and set two outdoor lounge chairs in the center of the room. A sunlamp and beach umbrella were placed over the chairs, offering sunlight and shade. He'd filled a kiddie wading pool with water; next to it stood a little tub of sand. Needless to say, Bob and Dorothy enjoyed a wonderful day at the "beach," talking, relaxing, and just being together.

It's easy to create an environment or mood if you think about your five senses. Plan things that will touch each sense. Just about everything you've experienced is recalled through your senses. A smell. A taste. Something you saw or heard. What can you do to include the senses as you create a mood?

HEARING. What do you hear that enables you to relax and enjoy the moment? Music? Waves crashing on the beach? Water rippling in a brook? A thunderstorm (one of my personal favorites)? And one of the fun things today is that you can often find CDs or tapes of sounds from nature for whatever mood you're attempting to create. When you can't go to the beach, find a tape of the sound of waves breaking on a beach. When it's been a while since you've experienced a great thunderstorm, a CD is the next-best thing. (And safer.)

One of the things I appreciate about playing music softly in the background is that it helps me to focus, to be less distracted. Perhaps hearing certain songs or composers instantly brings back special memories for you and your husband. Playing the music, recalling the memories, can re-create the emotions you felt before—helping to make this new moment special too.

SMELL. This is the one sense that often gets overlooked as you create a mood. But it's very important. Each of us has favorites smells, those that make us feel good, such as the fragrance of homemade vegetable soup or baking bread. Not necessarily "romantic" scents, but you get the idea. It's easy to include scent in your environment by the fragrance you wear. Add a touch of your cologne to a light bulb that will be turned on. The heat from the bulb will warm up the cologne and fill the room with fragrance. Candles come in wonderful fragrances—from gingerbread to jasmine. Even massage lotion is often scented. (I use vanilla-scented massage lotion on Friday nights. Each of the boys—and Tim, if he chooses—gets a massage before bed. In the future, when they smell vanilla, I know they'll remember those family Friday nights when we put everything else aside and spent time together.) Years from now familiar scents will still evoke good memories when my guys smell them again.

SIGHT. I'm a visual person, so this is an important part of the mood for me, but all of us enjoy beauty. Sunsets. Sunrises. A blazing fire. Soft candlelight. I enjoy the awesome beauty of mountains. Tim loves the crisp greenness of a pine forest. (That one adds scent, too.) Because Tim and I both enjoy the beauty of the outdoors, many of our dates are spent outside. We go hiking. We lie on a blanket under a starry sky. We sit by a yellow-red campfire or, in the winter, a fire in the fireplace.

Remember that you are a part of the visual beauty too. Take the time to make sure *you* look good. Too often married couples see each other at their worst. Baggy sweatpants. Oversized T-shirts. Uncombed hair. Of course, it's important that we love each other no matter what we look like, and that we feel comfortable just being ourselves. But when you plan special moments for just the two of you, take the time to look your best. Soak in a bubble bath. Lather on some scented lotion. Wear clothes that make you feel attractive. Take the time to make yourself extra-pretty. It will help your attitude, build your own anticipation, and add to the visual beauty of the moment.

TASTE. Many of our dates include food, even if it's just popcorn. So this is probably one of the easiest senses to include. (Of course, food isn't necessary for a great date.) One way Tim and I have had fun including taste in our time together has been trying new foods. We both had Chinese food for the first time together, and that particular restaurant became our favorite, even after we tried several other Chinese ones. A Middle Eastern restaurant provided quite the adventure as we tried food totally unfamiliar to us.

Sometimes our dates have been trips to the local farmers' market—a symphony of sights, sounds, and smells. There's always a lot of great food to try too. French fries. Tim likes his with vinegar. (Yuck!) Ice cream and waffles. (Also a favorite food at the beach.) Fresh produce. Batter-covered mushrooms. It's fun to add food to a date.

TOUCH. Touching is so very important. Hugging. Snuggling. Holding hands. I love to sit in church with Tim's arm around me. We still hold hands when we go for walks. It's important for men to realize that there are times women want to be held and to snuggle without it going any further. Touch doesn't have to lead to sex. Other good touches include back rubs or foot massages, or brushing the other person's hair. Tim and I occasionally slow dance in the privacy of our home, too. (I confess that he's not into it, but he knows how much I enjoy it.)

Ask your spouse, "What kind of touches make you feel good?" Then try it out. Hug to say hello. Hug to say good-bye. Hug to say "I love you" or "You did a great job." And never miss an opportunity to hold hands. Sit shoulder touching shoulder in church. If you each need to keep an eye on the kids, don't put them between you; put one or two on either side.

It's not necessary for a date to include all five senses, but thinking and planning to include as many as possible makes it all the more memorable. It doesn't take a lot of planning, either. Light a couple candles, put on a CD, snuggle close to each other on the sofa with a glass of some icy cold beverage. Or choose a restaurant that you both enjoy—something with a little more ambiance than fast food. (Though I did hear of a couple who dressed up in black tie and evening gown, took their own music and candles, and enjoyed an evening at McDonald's. No doubt they enjoyed the attention they got, too. Creativeness helps.)

MORE MOOD SETTERS. Other things add to the mood of a date, such as weather. A sunny day creates an entirely different mood than does a stormy night. A clear, starry night is different from a misty day on the beach or a foggy morning in your own back yard. Using different surroundings will create a new mood too. Outdoors. Indoors. Try out a room you've never spent a lot of time in before. One rainy night I took some music, candles, and a blanket up into the attic and created a cozy nook. The pitter-pat of rain on the roof added to the ambiance.

Where you spend your time together affects the mood too. Out under the stars, just the two of you, or at a baseball game with a thousand other people will create two entirely different moods. Try new places. Almost any place can be a great place for a date with the right attitude. We've met in the kitchen to bake cookies together, some of the best cookies I've—*we've*—ever made. I think the fun of doing it together helped. The other night we attended an outdoor concert and fireworks display—with a few thousand other people. We happened to be sitting next to the path people took to get back and forth. But even with that mob we still enjoyed each other. Listening to the music. Watching the fireworks. Wondering and chuckling about some of the clothes people wear today. Whether it's your home, a restaurant, a sporting event, or a quiet museum, the place you choose to explore together will add its own flavor to your time.

Be creative. Try new things, but include your favorites: favorite place, favorite scents. Colors. Foods. Music. Sounds.

A mood is created in the first five minutes of being together after being apart. So remember that no matter how much planning, or how perfect the setting, those first five minutes are crucial. Spend them relaxing. Saying "I love you." Kiss. Hug. Tell your spouse how much you're looking forward to being together. Compliment how your mate looks. Don't criticize, complain, or say, "I'm not sure this is going to be any fun." Such things will kill the mood. While it's not impossible to start over, it's easier to start off on the right foot.

Tim and I planned to spend our evening together Christmas shopping. Problem was, Tim hates shopping. He hates spending money. He dislikes crowds, and that evening he felt irritated by all the traffic around the mall. He was grumpy, and needless to say, I knew it wasn't going to be a great date. It was time to bail out. Not out of the date, but out of our plans. We skipped the toy store and headed for a favorite Mexican restaurant. An hour or two later, with full bellies and a more relaxed attitude, we finally braved the toy store and had as enjoyable a time as you can have spending money on toys in a crowded toy store.

If it seems obvious that your date is going to bomb, abandon it, and don't hold a grudge. If he's grumpy and not looking forward to the evening, postpone the time out. Change plans and do something else. Remember that the point of it all isn't to have a perfect date, with the perfect mood and environment. The goal is for you and your spouse to have time to talk, to grow closer, to continue to develop your friendship. While you hope that it will be fun and memorable—that's why you put the effort into creating the mood and planning something fun—you want it to be a time that strengthens your marriage, too.

CHAPTER 5

So What Do We Do?

The boys were asleep. Tim would be home any moment, and I wondered what he would think. It had taken a bit of work, but I was ready. Of course, I'd just had a terrible thought! What if he brought a friend home with him? You see, I was greeting him with a surprise—a hot tub evening.

No, I hadn't put in a hot tub. That would've been a bit too extravagant. Instead, I'd created my own. Moving the kitchen table and chairs out of the kitchen, I'd dragged the boys' wading pool up from the basement. (It was winter.) Then I'd started filling the tub with bubbles and hot water. The boys were still up, so I'd let them play in it for a while. (That had taken care of baths for the evening.) After they were tucked in and asleep, I'd scattered a dozen candles around the kitchen and added more hot water. When it was about time for Tim to arrive, I'd added myself. *That* was when I remembered that he'd recently brought a friend home after their meetings. I prayed that he'd be alone, and he was. It didn't take him long to join me.

For those of you who'd like to try this idea, let me warn you of one thing. While I'd planned the evening, I hadn't planned the morning after. How do you get the water out of a wading pool in the middle of your kitchen in the middle of winter? Tim, who has often rescued me from one of my plans, used a hose to syphon the water out the door. (I thought I was going to have to bail it by the bucket.)

Friends of ours tried their children's pool as a hot tub date too, with a little different results. They were enjoying the time, relaxing, laughing until they heard water dripping from the kitchen floor into the basement. Warning: check the wading pool for any holes or leaks before filling it. Having to mop up a wet basement dampened the fun of the evening.

The number of different things you can do on a date is limited only by your creativeness—or the ideas you get from friends and books. (Some of us may not be very creative, but we can try out ideas we read about or hear about. And often that's better, because the ideas are already tried and proven to work.)

What did you enjoy doing together before you were married? Replay dates from your "courting" days. Even then Tim and I spent a lot of Saturday afternoons hiking or walking at a park. We spent evenings in the pool at my parents' during the summer and watching *Quincy* on their couch in the winter. We'd go to the mall just to walk around or to sit and eat popcorn while watching people. Occasionally he'd come by my desk around lunchtime at work and invite me out to the Dairy Queen for a peanut buster parfait. While it's hard to find *Quincy* reruns, and my mom no longer has a pool, we still spend many of our dates hiking or walking—outdoors or at the mall. (Going to the mall to walk around has been a standby or a cop out, depending on which way you look at it.)

At a church at which I was sharing ideas for keeping romance in your marriage, a woman told how her husband had attempted to re-create one of their old dates. Years before, there was one particular restaurant they'd go to for shoe-fly pie. (It's a Lancaster County, Pennsylvania, specialty—a gooey molasses filling on the bottom, topped with a crumbly mixture of sugar and flour and spices.) On this particular day they headed to the restaurant to relive one of their old dates. Unfortunately, many years had passed, and the place had changed from a restaurant to a small store. But they still had their shoe-fly pie. Thinking they'd just have to buy a pie and take it home, they told the clerks about the times they'd come for a piece of pie and hot drink. Romantics at heart, I think, the people behind the counter sliced up some pie, found a hot drink, and made a little table for the couple. What a special memory! Not only for this couple, but probably for anyone else in the store at the time.

Talk with your spouse. Find out what dates stand out in her memory. Which ones would he love to re-create? Then try it again. If it was fun once, it might be fun twice. Besides, just reminiscing will be worth the time spent, reminding you of the fun of young love.

Re-creating old dates may be fun, but trying new things is great too. Ideas aren't too hard to find. Talk to friends. Find out what they do. Ask around. What's been fun for others? Brainstorm with your spouse things you'd enjoy doing together. He might have some ideas you'd never think of. It's fun to make a list of all the things you could do together, even if you never try them all. (And some of them you might not really want to try.)

Try new restaurants, not just the kind you always choose. Try a new kind of food. Never been to a Thai restaurant? Look one up in the phone book. We tried our first Vietnamese restaurants together, and it has become our favorite place to eat.

Do things you've always wanted to but never tried, such as parking. Tim and I never went parking when we were dating, but now that we've been married, it's been a fun date once in a while. (OK, we never actually leave the driveway, but the car was still parked.) Slow dance by candlelight in the privacy of your own home. Go wading in a creek together. Stargaze on a blanket on a starry summer night. Set up a TV and VCR in your garage and create your own drive-in movie. Don't forget the popcorn!

I'd wanted to do it, and once before went so far as to reserve a room at a quaint bed and breakfast that had a private Jacuzzi in each room. But that hadn't worked out, and we had had to cancel. This time would be different. My plans were all made. The hotel room was reserved—a room that opened directly into the pool area. The car was packed with our suitcases and a picnic lunch, plus a few more things for breakfast. One of Tim's friends who lived in the area was going to meet us for dinner at a favorite restaurant. There was only one thing left to do—get Tim into the car.

Kidnapping your mate can be an adventure. You can do it for a day or a weekend—as I did for Tim's birthday trip. He thought he was going to Gettysburg to help me check out a hotel I planned to use for our next women's retreat. (And we did check out the hotel—better than he thought we were going to. We stayed there!) He didn't know that the trunk of the car held not only the picnic lunch I told him we'd eat on the battlefield, but also everything we needed to spend the night. When we got to the hotel I told him what was up. He took it all in stride, and we had a great weekend.

But you don't have to plan a whole weekend. Even kidnapping your spouse from work for a long lunch is fun too. Just be sure you know his schedule. Tim's enjoyed the occasional times I've dropped by his office and invited him to eat lunch with me. I always pack his lunch, so he grabs it and we head to a nearby park to walk and kiss, and hope the park rangers are out to lunch too. It just takes a little preplanning and sometimes the help of a friend or coworker. The element of surprise lends to the fun of the day. And your anticipation makes it exciting for you, too. (I didn't realize how much the boys enjoyed my "kidnapping" Tim until a friend gave me red handcuffs with white hearts on them as a joke. Zack took one look at them and exclaimed, "Mom, you can use them to kidnap Dad!")

Just getting away from the house and the phones, and being unable to see everything that needs done, helps. Make plans to spend an entire day away from home. Check out the new cars and trucks in your town's car lots. Dream a little. Pretend to be tourists in your own community. With a little planning you can take a tour through local "attractions," such as a potato chip factory or your city newspaper.

One day Tim and I loaded up our bikes and spent the day biking in a cute village nearby. It was a Sunday afternoon, and there were several open houses in new developments. We parked our bikes and strolled through homes we could never afford. But it was fun. Attend a local ball game. Many community parks have ball fields with local teams playing. Cheer on the visiting team together, or each of you cheer a different team.

We often think of dates being at nighttime, and you can think of a lot of great nighttime dates. A candlelight picnic in the backyard. Skinny-dipping in your pool, the one surrounded by the high wooden fence. Picking up a pizza just before the pizza shop closes and eating it while watching old movies. (This was one of our favorite Saturday night dates before we had kids. These days I have a hard time staying up past 10:00.) But there are a lot of great daytime dates, too. Get up early and fix her breakfast in bed. Have a picnic in the kids' treehouse—just the two of you. Build a snowman together. Go for a walk in the rain. Go to the zoo or somewhere that's traditionally for kids, but don't take yours along.

Dates can also be a way of making something you don't particularly enjoy doing fun, such as doing a chore together. Baking cookies or fixing dinner together. Sometimes when Tim's outside working on the house or car, I'll go out and just sit and watch. Of course, I don't sit there quietly, so it often becomes a great time for us to talk. (The kids don't usually come around when there's work being done. They're afraid they might be asked to help.)

Dates can take a lot of work or require very little planning. Surprise him by stopping by work in the evening and taking him out to dinner. Reminisce with old photos. Take a bubble bath or candlelight shower together. Share an ice-cream cone or milk shake—two straws, please! Invest in a pair of satin sheets, and spread them with flower petals or spray lightly with perfume. Pamper her for a day—don't let her do any work. Make it a day of relaxation and being cared for. Fix a theme dinner; our favorite to fix at home is Mexican. Eat by candlelight—even if it's leftovers. Read a book together. Take a class together—something you both want to learn. Discover a new hobby together.

Do something that your spouse enjoys doing even if it's not your favorite thing. Attend his favorite sporting event. Surprise him with tickets to see his favorite team. Go with her to the ballet or a concert. Go to a garden show, a dog show, or the farm exhibits at the state fair. I always wanted to walk barefoot, holding hands, wearing bulky sweaters on a cool, drizzly beach. When a company Tim was working for part-time had meetings in Hilton Head, South Carolina, we got our chance. One afternoon during a break in meetings and activities the conditions were perfect for our walk alone on that misty beach. We walked, holding hands, and wrote love notes in the sand. And *that's* the memory that stands out from all the other nice things that happened that weekend.

Do you know your spouse's fantasy date? What would she love to do? Try it. Make it fun—it's a matter of attitude. Tim has attended craft shows with me. Not because he's interested in crafts, but because he's interested in me. Sharing your mate's interests helps you to get to know each other better.

Remember that the activity you're doing together isn't as important as the fact that you're together. That you're building a stronger friendship. Talking. Laughing. Having fun. Building memories. Don't be afraid to be silly. And don't be afraid that a date might bomb. Maybe it won't be as fun as you'd like, but that's OK. You're not trying to have great dates—you're attempting to build a great marriage.

Enjoy each other.

CHAPTER 6

Showing Love

One of the most important things in a marriage—at least for many women—is love. Feeling loved. Showing love. And while as we grow older we realize that love isn't as much a feeling as it is an action, you and I still need to know that we're loved. Cherished. Cared about. And the way we know we're loved is through tangible expressions of that love. What we do and say speak volumes. How can you help your spouse feel loved?

Often it's the little things that mean a lot.

Hold hands.

Lay your hand on his leg while he's driving.

Interrupt him, when he's talking, with a compliment and a kiss. (This works especially well when you're bored.)

Whisper something romantic or suggestive in her ear in a crowded room.

Leave a suggestive message on your answering machine.

Leave a message for her at the front desk of a restaurant or the service desk at a store and have her paged to receive it. (It's best to write the message down and put it in a sealed envelope.) Make a "treasure hunt" of sorts for her to "discover" the treasure of you. Cut "footprints" out of construction paper and write little notes on them. Then leave them out so that they leave a trail to where you are when she arrives home. Or write clues that lead on a trail to a romantic setting—at home, or if you're more adventurous, let the clues lead him through your area to dinner at a romantic restaurant.

Give her coupons for herself. Around Valentine's Day you can often purchase coupon books at bookstores and department stores. But if you can't, make up your own. Include coupons for massages, special foods, time for herself, a day with you to do whatever she wants. Be creative.

Place a love note ad in the local paper. Many newspapers have Valentine's ads in February. Tim still carries in his wallet the ad I placed in the paper 17 years ago.

Fill his car with balloons while he's at work. Include a card. The kids really enjoyed helping with this one—blowing them up and then stuffing them into the car. I appreciated their help because I have a terrible time blowing up balloons. (And including them in on the act helps them to have fun and teaches them how to show love to others, too.)

Make a banner welcoming him home or proclaiming your love for her and stick it in the front yard. Tie it to a tree. Put it in the hands of a snowman you and the kids have built. I never realized how much my neighbors enjoyed our banners for Tim until one woman asked me when I was going to leave another note up for my husband. She enjoyed reading them when she drove past the house. The banners were always something I did with the kids. We made the banner (I did the writing; when they were small they did the artwork). We built the snowman together and chose where to hang it. The boys enjoyed "working" with me to surprise Daddy. And Tim always enjoyed the welcome home. (Though I admit that he always took the banner down immediately. Most of them are hanging in the back of his closet.)

Go out of your way to meet her when she arrives home from work or a meeting. Take the kids for a walk down the road to meet her. (Hopefully, she has a regular route of coming home—you wouldn't want to be waiting there while she drove home a different way.) When you see her car, wave and jump up and down. Then hitch a ride home with her. This teaches the children that a parent's arrival home is an exciting event to be celebrated.

Make an encouragement calendar. Write 31 encouraging notes for your spouse on 3" x 5" cards. Write notes that tell what you like or appreciate about your mate. Include mushy love notes. Punch holes through the top corners and tie them together with a ribbon.

Leave little notes everywhere. Write down reminders of your love. What you enjoy about him. The things you appreciate most about her. That you miss him. Remind her of your anticipation of coming home to her. I love to do this when I go away for a weekend. I tuck notes in pockets of clothes I think Tim might wear. Hide them in shoes. In cereal boxes. In the freezer. Tape them to the toothpaste. Wherever he might look. One time I even came across Post-its that were shaped like lips. Often I tuck love notes in his lunch box. Or mail a steamy love note or cute card to his office. Or e-mail him a reminder of my love and that I'm thinking of him.

Tanya tucked in a special box of Cracker Jacks in

Loren's lunch. She'd carefully opened the bottom of the box, swiped the prize, and enclosed her own special "prize," something that had meaning for both of them. Then she fixed the box so that it didn't look tampered with. Not only did Loren enjoy his Cracker Jack treat, but the guys he worked with enjoyed the surprise, too.

Celebrate life's little victories and accomplishments. Tim brought flowers and ice-cream sandwiches—the kind made from cookies—home to celebrate an accomplishment with one of my books. I sneaked a peek in the envelope that arrived from the board with whom he'd taken a test to make sure he'd passed; then the boys and I headed out to buy a briefcase and for food for a special supper. Life is short. Celebrate every moment you can together.

Take the time to find out what makes your spouse feel loved. One of my friends took the time to write down a list of the things her husband could do to make her feel loved. He keeps the list handy and often picks something from it to do. He knows that everything on the list is a surefire way of making her feel special—she wrote the list. She appreciates his efforts, and is feeling more loved.

In his wonderful book *The Five Love Languages* Gary Chapman says that each of us "hears" love in different ways. And if we learn our spouse's "love language" we will be able to "speak" love to him in a way that makes him truly feel loved. His book shares how to determine both your love language and that of your mate's, and gives ideas of how to "speak" love to your spouse. Chapman gives five ways in which we may hear or speak love.

PHYSICAL TOUCH. People whose love language is physical touch feel loved through touch. Saying love through touch include: massages, holding hands, snuggling, brushing their hair or rubbing their head, kissing good night. One couple said that they kiss every time they say "Amen" after their prayers. Making physical contact is important and is simple. Rubbing his shoulders as he sits at the table. Giving her a foot massage while she sits on the sofa reading a book. Holding hands while walking.

GIFTS. Others feel most loved when they receive a gift. You can leave little surprises on her pillow, in his car. The gifts don't have to be expensive. Just a little something to show that you were thinking of them. Gifts can be homemade or store-bought and as simple as a package of peanuts.

Emma wanted her husband to send her flowers. It was something that made her feel loved and was important to her. So she went to Bob and told him, "It makes me feel loved to get roses from you. Could you send them to me from time to time?" He responded, "How often would you like to have them?" When she answered, "Once a month would be nice," he wrote it down in his calendar. On the fifteenth of every month Emma receives roses from Bob. It might not be spontaneous, but it's still a reminder that he loves her.

ENCOURAGING WORDS. To those with the love language of encouraging words, what you say means a lot. Speak words of encouragement often. Tell her she did a great job. That you're proud of her. Let him know how much you appreciate his help with the kids or around the house. Tell her she looks pretty. Whistle at him when he walks into the room. Thank him for working hard to provide for and take care of the family. Tell her that she's doing a great job as a mom. Always thank him when he does something that you appreciate—it'll make him feel good and be an encouragement to do it again. Send her an encouraging note at work. Fill a container with notes and tell him to take one every time he needs an encouraging word.

ACTS OF SERVICE. To show love to someone whose love language is acts of service, keep an eye out for things that they'd like or need done. Weed the garden. Mow the grass. Help her put that computer desk together. Do those errands he's going to need to do this weekend. What are those things she's always wanting done around the house? If you keep putting them off and her love language is acts of service, she may not be feeling very loved or cared about.

Sally feels cared about when people help her. Acts of service. She remembers struggling in her backyard, attempting to trim branches from several trees. The saw wasn't cooperating. Tony came home while she was still working on the second tree, and even though he needed to change and get to a ball game he took the time to trim the remaining trees for her. "I didn't mean to hold him up from his game," Sally said. "He was working a lot of overtime and the ball games were a real outlet for all the extra stress and time cooped up in the office. I was determined to do the job myself. But I appreciated his help so much. I knew that he cared about me more than anything else."

QUALITY TIME. For those who hear love through quality time, it's not the time factor as much as it is the connection at a deep level. This is my love language. I *need* for Tim to spend time with me. And not just for us to be in the same room at the same time, but for us to connect on a heart level. When our lives get busy and we don't get time to sit down and talk or go for a walk or have our monthly date—which happens often—I start feeling lonely. Sometimes unloved. I get irritable. Easily discouraged. I need to spend time with my husband. I need to connect with him. It doesn't take much. After dinner Tim and I often spend a few minutes sitting at the table talking. The dishes can wait. (And if they can't, assign the job to the kids.) Or we'll go for a walk in the evening while the boys ride their bikes.

These days Tim is working on the house every night after dinner, usually until after dark. By the time he cleans up his work area and takes a shower we're both tired and ready for bed. So while I'm rarely any help (I have offered), I go out and talk to him while he works. I've sat up on the scaffolding or hung out wherever he's working. It's time for us to reconnect. To talk. To listen. To be friends.

Sometimes it's hard to squeeze in time together. There's so much that has to be done. But even little bits of time here and there—eating breakfast together, talking in the dark after the lights are turned off, connecting via the telephone for a few minutes during the day—helps. We have to make the time even when we can't find it. The quality of our marriages depend on it.

Knowing that different things make different people feel more loved also tells us that you and I attempt to show our love in different ways too. Gary Chapman writes that we often "speak" the same love language that we "hear."

There have been times in our marriage that I've wondered if Tim loved me. And if he did, why did he do some of the things he did? Why didn't he *show* me that he loved me?

Such as fighting my hurt feelings every time I was getting ready to go away for a weekend women's retreat. Instead of being inside sharing those last moments with me, Tim would be out in the driveway changing the oil in the car. Was the car really that important? But, thanks to a Christian radio program, I realized that *the car* wasn't important. *I* was. Tim was saying, "Tami, I love you. I love you so much that I want to make sure that you're safe. So I'm checking out the car. Changing the oil. Making sure you have everything you need in the car. I don't want anything to happen to you, because you're precious to me."

He didn't actually say those words. *(That* might have helped me to get the message sooner.) But I realized that that was exactly what his actions were saying. Sometimes to hear someone saying I love you, we have to look past what we'd like and hear what they're saying in their own way. We have our own expectations of what love looks like and sounds like. But each of us is unique. Each of us has our own way of saying "I love you!"

I love doing all the little, fun things. Planning surprises. From big things like kidnapping him to small things like including a deli dill pickle in his lunch just because I know he enjoys it. He's been working on the house so much lately that I've offered and given a lot of back rubs when he's through for the day. (These also give me the opportunity to talk to him without his walking away!) Just a minute ago, when I thought of the lip-shaped Post-its, I grabbed one and wrote a quick note, leaving it on his workbench to find when he comes in to saw the next piece of siding. My mind is constantly running, so the ideas aren't hard to come by.

Tim shows his love more by what he does. Taking care of me. Providing for our family. Every nail he hammers into this house is one way he says "I love you!" He could be playing or relaxing. Or pursuing something he enjoys. But instead he's working to make a nicer place for our family. And every inch is as perfect as he can make it. (And he is actually enjoying the work.) If I didn't understand that this is his way of showing love, I could easily get resentful of the time and distraction. Watch your spouse;

look for the ways he shows his love.

Steve isn't so great with working around the house. Taking on a project the size of ours is unthinkable to him. Even small projects just aren't his forte. But Steve shows his love in other ways. Helping with the kids. Encouraging words. Taking his wife out for dinner at the end of a hard day. He does all he can to try to make her life easier. And she appreciates it. She knows that she's loved. He'd do anything he could for her.

Sometimes it may be difficult to show your spouse that you love him. That's when your commitment "for better or for worse, for richer or poorer, in sickness and in health, till death do us part" means the most. When you're hurt or angry, or just don't feel as if you love him anymore—and those times can be a normal part of married life—your commitment to love no matter what is revealed to be real or not. Are you really willing to show love when you don't feel loving? When times are tough and he's not any fun to be around. You're angry and just want to scream. Or so hurt that you're thinking about walking away from it all.

It's not hard to love when life is easy. When you're getting along fine. Life is good. Pleasant. You're both happy. It doesn't take a commitment to love when everything is wonderful.

But when the bills are larger than the paycheck. When his words cut your heart like a knife. Or her silence kills a little bit of you every time you see her. When walking out the door seems the easiest thing to do. Or even when it's not such a big problem, you've just had a little argument. Or he's hurt your feelings again. *That's* when you see what your commitment is made of. That's when love is most needed.

There have been times Tim has made me angry or hurt my feelings. Times when I've felt as if my spirit has been crushed once too often. These are opportunities for the devil to whisper, "Why don't you just leave him? He doesn't really love you anyway." At times my longing to be loved was so great that it was practically unbearable, but I felt nothing but silence.

I can't say that I've always responded with love. I've pouted. I've sulked. I've said my share of angry words. Sarcastic words. And cried a lot of tears. But each time, I realized that I had made a commitment to this man. And that deep down, I loved him. That I wanted to be with him. That somehow I had to get through the hurt.

Only God can help us love when we don't feel loving. He alone can help us to give love when we have nothing to give. When we don't even want to give. And God has taught me a couple things about what to do when I don't feel loved or like loving Tim.

TELL THE DEVIL TO GET OUT OF HERE. I remember the moment vividly. Tim had done something to hurt me. I'm sure it wasn't intentional; it rarely is. But that didn't soften the pain. I was angry, I was hurt, and I was screaming inside. But on the outside I was taking the boys to school and driving home to tackle the day's project. Inside there was a battle going on. The devil knew what had happened and how I'd be feeling. That's when he began to whisper his suggestions: "Why don't you just leave him? Go home and pack your clothes. Pick up the kids after school and hit the road. He won't miss you."

I entertained the thoughts. Toying with them in my mind. Almost agreeing with them. That's when I realized what was happening. What had happened many times in the past. And I knew with a new strength that I never wanted to walk away from my marriage. That I loved this man too much. And that he loved me. These difficult moments were just part of two imperfect people living together. Especially a part of two people living together who are such opposites. I knew what I had to do. I knew that I couldn't think these thoughts. I almost shouted in the car, "Get out of here, Satan. I love this man, and I am *never* walking away from this marriage." From then on, I've chosen not to listen to the devil's whisperings. When I hear those familiar tunes, I tell him to get away. I am in this to stay.

Remember that you are involved in a very real battle. One that you can't see, but that is very real. The devil wants to destroy your marriage. He wants to destroy all marriages. It's one way to destroy people, families, and lives. He doesn't want you living happily ever after. He wants you miserable. Recognize his voice, and recognize God's voice. Then any other will stand out in an instant. God will never ask you to do anything contrary to His Word or will. If it's not God, don't listen.

LET MY EXPECTATIONS BE TO GOD ALONE. This is actually found in a verse in the Bible, Psalm 62:5: "My soul, wait silently for God alone, for my expectation is from Him" (NKJV). I had a lot of expectations of Tim. I wanted him to come home at the end of the day and listen to me. Really listen. I wanted him to make me feel loved. At times, without even realizing it, I wanted him to make me feel good about myself. I wanted him to want to spend time with me. To plan dates and invite me out. Surprise me. I wanted him to know what I needed. Whether it was a back rub or time out from the boys. And then I wanted him to meet that need. I think I even wanted him to read my mind. (And sometimes I absolutely didn't want him to be able to!)

One day I was moaning about Tim to my friend Janet. That's when she shared this difficult passage with me. She told me that I shouldn't *expect* anything from Tim. I needed to let all my expectations be of God. That was hard. Tim was someone I could see. He was my husband. Didn't I have a right to expect certain things? You may agree or disagree with the idea. But I've slowly learned to give all my expectations to God. It makes those times Tim does meet my needs so much sweeter! When I'm lonely, instead of expecting Tim to fill that void, I go to God. He may give me a song, a friend, or time with Tim, but He knows exactly what's best to fill that void. (And sometimes it's time with Him that I needed all along.)

When I'm feeling unloved and I just want someone to care, I go to God. He has a zillion ways to show love. It can be through people, even many times through Tim. But it might be through nature, through something I see or hear or read. Taking my expectations to God ensures that my needs will be met and that I won't be angry with Tim over an expectation or need he doesn't even know about. And it gives me the freedom to love Tim unconditionally. Without regard to what I might get back or should get back. I don't withhold love because he hasn't met my needs. I take those needs to God and love Tim just because I love him.

LOVE IS AN ACTION, NOT A FEELING. Sometimes I don't feel loving. I'm hurt or too tired or too empty myself. I don't want to show love; I want to feel it. Or I don't want to be loving, because of the anger or pain. That's the time I need to do something loving for Tim. Action—even when the feeling isn't there. The feelings will follow. Many times the feelings have come very quickly once I acted loving.

One time in particular when I was angry with Tim stands out. I was feeling a lot of things, but none of them were loving. But I'd decided ahead of time that the next time I got angry with him, I'd do something loving for him. So I did. I went outside, started the lawn mower, and took my frustrations out on the front lawn. By the time the lawn was mowed, I was feeling better. God and I had talked about the anger. The physical exertion had been a good vent for my steam. And I liked seeing a fresh-mowed lawn. (I love the yard when it's nicely mowed.) When I put the mower away, I was ready to go find my husband. Not to give him a piece of my mind, but to give him a kiss. And a hug.

Doing something loving for Tim when I'm angry or hurt often reminds me how very much I do love this man. When I look at the situation through love, it often doesn't seem so bad. I can see his side a little more. God even often convicts me of my part in it all. It's rarely just one person's fault. We usually both play a part in it.

If I am truly committed to my marriage, I will act loving no matter what.

This doesn't mean that you shouldn't talk about what you're feeling. Or that you should just bottle your feelings up and go on with life—pretending to be happy and loving. I never pretended. Tim knew exactly how I felt when I went out to mow. But while I was mowing, while I was acting loving, God and I were able to work through my hurt and anger. I saw some of my part. I forgave Tim of his. When I was calmer, and feeling more loving, Tim and I were able to talk about what had happened without the intense feelings of the moment. Calmly, rationally, I could then tell him what he did or said and why it hurt.

Never bottle up your feelings or pretend that they aren't there. Bottling up your feelings isn't showing love. It will drain love from you. Eventually you will explode. And the damage caused may be irreparable. Talk about it. But wait till you're both calm. Pray about it, on your own and together. Ask God to convict you of what you may have done wrong—how you could've added to the situation. Ask God to give you love and forgiveness for your mate.

Honest, open communication is a must in any marriage. This means talking about the good stuff—the day-to-day events, as well as those difficult times. Learning to talk about the conflict can be difficult. Some of us prefer to wait silently for it all to pass over. Others like to yell and scream and get it all out. Some can't stop the tears. But we have to talk about it. If we don't, it doesn't go away. It becomes a brick in a wall growing between us. Every time we allow another anger or hurt to be swallowed and not discussed, another brick goes up in the wall. And that's another lesson God taught me.

In the beginning of our marriage neither Tim nor I were any good at working through difficult times. Arguments. Disagreements. Hurt feelings. Anger. We had never seen our parents work through any of these things. Neither of us really remembered our parents arguing. At least not in front of us. There might have been silences, but we never saw them talk out a problem.

So when we had our first "fight" (Tim prefers to call them "discussions"), we didn't know what to do. I retreated and pouted. He stormed out and was silent. Things were pretty quiet around our house for a couple days until it passed over. Slowly we began talking again. Not about "it," but talking. The incident was pushed down somewhere inside. Trouble was, it kept wanting to pop back up. Along with other things we were silently stuffing down.

Somewhere along the line, after years of being married,

we learned that we had to stick with it and talk it out no matter how long it took or how many tears. (The tears were mine, of course.) Tough lesson. Hard to do at times. We both hate conflict. There were many times Tim didn't want to talk because it was so painful. Because he hated that I ended up crying. But I kept reminding him that we had to work it out. That the tears and hurt might be a part of the process, but we had to continue on.

These days it's much easier to work through the anger and hurt. I don't get hurt and want to walk away. Instead I want to show Tim that I still love him by working through the problem. Working through a problem is another way of showing love. You're saying, "I love you enough to take care of all the things that might hurt our relationship."

It's become easier for us to talk calmly. We've learned to talk until both of us are satisfied that we've been understood and that the problem is resolved in some way. It requires that we both listen and that we both share honestly. Often it means staying up late. But showing love in this way may be one of the most important things we can do for our love. Being committed no matter what. No matter what the pain, the time of night or the tears, we're going to work through everything that comes our way—together.

Showing love is fun. Doing those little things each day that tell your spouse "I love you." Showing love can also be difficult. It's remaining committed to the relationship no matter what you're feeling. It's acting on the commitment of love even when the feeling of love isn't there. But showing love is part of the stitching that holds together the fabric of your marriage.

CHAPTER 7

What Do We Talk About?

Finally! At last Jeannie and Gary had managed to get a night out together. The atmosphere was wonderful, for Gary had found a quaint Mexican restaurant complete with a strolling guitar player. Created inside the restaurant itself was an outdoor café straight from Monterey. Lights. Trees. Flowers. Small booths built into alcoves along the side of the room. The tortilla chips were warm and salty, the salsa fresh and spicy. Huge, heated dinner plates arrived with steaming Spanish rice and beans and the largest cheese and vegetable burritos they'd ever seen.

For dessert they shared fried ice cream crowned with chocolate syrup and whipped cream dribbling down into little pools on the plate. The waiter even put two cherries on the top. The atmosphere and the meal created a perfect date. There was just one problem.

Jeannie and Gary didn't have a thing to talk about.

They'd promised each other that they wouldn't talk about the bills, work, or problems with the kids. Nothing unpleasant or difficult was allowed. So what did that leave? They sat in silence. Looking around. Smiling at each other once in a while. Neither had any idea where or how to begin conversation if they didn't talk about the same old things they rehashed over supper every night.

Once you're out with your sweetie, just the two of you, what *do* you talk about? How do you have a conversation that helps you know each other better? When you think about the goals for your marriage, it likely includes conversation that goes deep to your hearts. You long to be true soul mates as well as best friends. To know each other intimately and completely. *How* do you learn to share from your heart?

First, realize that what you say is only a small part of what people hear. What you say is far more than the words you choose. Content is only 7 percent of what people hear, while 38 percent of your communication is tone of voice. How do you say what you say? Many times it hasn't been Tim's words that hurt me, but his tone of voice. It's been the way he said it that hurt. And at times I can be very sarcastic. Again, it's the way I say it, not the words I say.

Listen to yourself. Smile when you talk. Even on the telephone smiling makes a difference in your tone of voice.

The biggest part of communication is your body language, for 55 percent of what you are really saying is conveyed that way. How are you sitting? Are you facing and looking at the person speaking to you? Do you make eye contact? (Women are more comfortable making eye contact than are men.) Are your arms crossed in front of you, or are you relaxed and open? Do you occasionally reach out and touch the person you're talking or listening to? A touch often speaks volumes when words don't mean anything. A hug says "I care about you." A slap screams anger. A gentle touch on the arm while looking the person in the eyes says "I'm listening to you. I really care about you." When a friend or loved one is facing a huge loss it's hard to know what to say. Mere words seem empty in the face of tragedy. That's when a hug says it all.

Your words, your tone of voice, and your body language are most important when you talk with your spouse. And while you need to be careful about your words (and we'll talk about that later), you also should watch your tone of voice and pay attention to your body language. What are you really saying? Do your tone and body language match the words coming out of your mouth?

"I hate it when I ask Bill how I look and he says 'You look great, hon' without even looking up from the TV," Stacey confided to a friend. But there's nothing wrong with what Bill said. Most women love to be told that they look great. But when Bill doesn't drag his eyes from the TV to look at his wife, his words are meaningless. "I feel as though he can't be bothered. He doesn't really care how I look."

"The other night Dan and I were having a discussion. We both wanted something different. I tried to explain my point of view, to help him understand what I was thinking. He said that he understood, but I don't think he did. He sat stiffly in his chair with his arms crossed, looking angry. I don't think he heard or cared what I had to say—even though he said that he did. He surely didn't look like it," shares another wife.

"When I get home in the evening, I enjoy sharing my day with Emma," Don says. "I want to tell her how my work went and ask her about her day. But I don't know that she cares if I tell her about my day or not. She just keeps on with whatever she was doing when I walked in—filling the dishwasher, checking the mail, looking through a magazine. She stops long enough to kiss me hello and then goes right back to what she was doing. Never looks up. After a while I get the message and go find something else to do. I wish she'd just take a couple minutes to stop and listen."

You're busy. I'm busy. We're all busy. When we finally get home at the end of a long work day, our work isn't over. There's still another whole world of things that must be done. You may tend to just jump right in and get started for no one else is going to do it if you don't. Right? But remember that your marriage is more important than the work. Dinner can wait a couple of minutes. The housework isn't going anywhere, but your spouse may. If your husband or wife wants to talk to you, give them your complete attention.

"But I am listening," complains Emma. "I'm listening while I work. I can do two things at one time. I could tell you everything Don said."

She may be listening. You may be listening. Tim told me he was listening the other night as I told him stories from the window while he worked on the siding—but I couldn't tell if he was. (I believe him. And I knew he had to get the siding done.) But if your body language isn't showing that you're listening, you're not. For your spouse is "listening" to your body language.

So how do you show you're really listening?

Make eye contact. Eye contact shows that you value the other person. That you're hearing what they're saying. We need to make eye contact—not just when the other person is talking, but when we're talking too.

Stop what you're doing and face the person who's talking. Put down the newspaper and look her in the eyes. Set the laundry down, or stop doing the dishes. To really listen, you need to be focused, not distracted. Respond in ways that will enable the conversation to continue. My friend Sue teaches a class on active listening. She shares several great tools on how to listen more effectively.

PLAY BACK WHAT YOU HEARD THE OTHER PERSON SAY.
Gary Smalley, in his book *Making Love Last Forever,* says that this is similar to what the "speaker" does at the drive-through at fast-food restaurants. You give your order; they repeat it back to you. Then you let them know if they got it right or not. We can do this as we listen to each other, too.

Carrie says, "I'm not sure a trip to Idaho would be a good idea right now. It might be hard to take the time off work, and there are things that need done around here. Besides, who's going to take care of the dog?"

Geoff plays back what he's heard. "So you don't want to go to Idaho with me for a week."

This gives Carrie an opportunity to let him know if he's heard what she's really said. "No, that's not it. I'd like to go; it's just that there's so much to do and the trip is so soon."

"So what you're saying is that you'd like to go, but there are a lot of details that would need to be taken care of. And you're not sure how you would get them all done."

"Yes. That's it. I love to go away with you on your trips, but this one is on such short notice. I'm just not sure if it's a good time."

If Geoff hadn't played back what his wife said and had the opportunity to understand what she really meant, he might have walked away feeling rejected that she didn't want to go with him. But it wasn't that Carrie didn't want to go. It was that there was so much to do in order to take the trip that she didn't think she could manage it all. Playing back what we hear allows the person to clarify what they say. It opens the door for both people to understand. The one playing back can more clearly understand what's being said. And the one talking will feel more open to continue sharing when they know they're being understood.

IDENTIFY FEELINGS. Read between the lines. What is the other person feeling? This is similar to playing back words, but you "play back" the feelings instead. "So you're feeling frustrated that your boss assigned the job to the other person?" "You're disappointed that the evening didn't turn out the way you had hoped?" Again, it opens the door for the person to respond, "Yes, that's exactly how I felt," or "No, I wasn't really frustrated. I . . ." The more you attempt to understand, the more willing people are to talk, and the deeper the conversation can go. (This applies to more than marriage. It's good for friendships and business relationships, too.)

DON'T TRY TO SOLVE THE PROBLEM. JUST *LISTEN*. Usually people don't want their problems solved; they just want someone to listen. That's why many women go to a girlfriend when they want to talk. Women are usually better listeners than men. They interrupt less; they show compassion and sympathy. And they don't always try to solve problems.

Most men are problem solvers by nature. That's the way God made them. And that's good. We need that. But many times men get in trouble—whether they realize it or not—because they try to explain to their wives what they've done wrong and how they could do it better, or what they should do about it. And all the wife wanted was someone to understand, to hold them, and to listen. There have been times I've shared something with Tim, and then gone to

Tanya with the same thing. I went to Tanya because I needed someone to understand—not to tell me that I'm too sensitive or take things personally (which I can be and can do, but that's not what I needed to hear at the time).

There's a better way than trying to solve the problem on the spot! After playing back your spouse's words and identifying the feelings behind them, ask questions that will lead him or her to solutions. When you do both of those, your spouse will feel as though you understand and will be more open to your help in problem solving. But don't *tell* her what to do. Help her to figure out what she can do. You might ask, "So what do you think you could do about this? Do you have any ideas?"

Again, this works well with friends and family, too.

When our son Zack was younger, he had a problem with anger. It was easy for him to fly off the handle at school and hit someone. We talked about it, and I asked "So what are some things you think you could do next time Gabriel makes you mad?" Together we began to list possibilities. I didn't tell him what to do, but I did ask questions. "Do you think you could walk away? Could you count to 10 and then tell him that you're angry? Could you find a ball and throw it as far as you can instead of hitting Gabe?"

Zack made a list of the things he thought he could do and planned out how to respond next time he got angry. The solutions were his, not mine. *He* decided what he could do, planning in advance. I only guided him. If I'd commanded, "Next time Gabriel makes you angry, just walk away" Zack might have dug in his heels. Not because he didn't want to get control of his temper, but because we're more likely to change our behavior when it is our decision. Zack thought it through, and he decided. The solution was his—not mine.

Don't tell your mate what to do. Don't tell him how he

caused the problem. Or how he's handling it. That's not listening. Try to understand what she's saying. How he's feeling. Then encourage her as she works through to a solution.

Listening is a very important part of our communication. Good listeners are hard to come by. It's been said many times that God gave us two ears and one mouth so we would listen twice a much as we talk. But talk is important too. What can you do to enable better conversations with your spouse?

KEEP IT UPBEAT. We've said it before. Have a time to talk about the problems and stresses, but make sure you also set a time to talk about positive things. Fun things. Conversations that will help you get to know each other better—grow your relationship.

HAVE THE RIGHT MIND-SET. If you think it's not going to be fun, it won't be. If you expect it to be crowded and miserable, it will be. Think positive. Go with great expectations.

When Tim and I went to a concert and fireworks display over the Fourth of July, we knew to expect huge crowds. Many of our friends had warned us that the traffic afterward would be horrendous, with up to an hour delay. We went knowing that, but we didn't let it deter us. We went expecting delays and backed-up traffic, so we planned on waiting. We also expected it to be hot and crowded. But we also expected to have fun. To enjoy the music. To be awed by the fireworks. To be deafened by the actual cannons during the *1812 Overture.*

And it all happened, just as we expected. But we enjoyed it. We found a front-row seat on the grass. Took plenty of water. Sat near the cannons so we could watch them go off. People-watched. Talked. Enjoyed the music and the enthusiasm of the symphony director. The cannons were deafening, and a magnificent addition to the symphony. The fireworks were awesome, amazing, incredible. When it was over we walked back to our car with several hundred other people. Then we waited. We didn't attempt the traffic, which was backed up for about a half hour. We talked some more. We didn't get irritated by the delay or the fact that once we could get into the flow of traffic we were going only five miles an hour. We knew what to expect and made the best of it. Remember that you usually find what you're looking for. Expect the best.

COMMUNICATE OPENLY. Say what you're thinking. He can't read your mind. Don't expect her to know unless you tell her.

If you don't want to do something, say so. Things have a way of coming out sooner or later, and later usually isn't better. Even discussions or arguing can lead to a deeper intimacy. I don't know how many late-night "discussions" have caused Tim and me to talk openly and deeply. By the end—despite how hard it was to get through—we felt closer to each other. Share what you're thinking and feeling. What you want. Your hopes and dreams. Talk about your day. Husbands and wives spend so much time apart. You need to talk to keep each other informed about what's happening in your lives. What's important to the other person.

Often it's easier for women to talk openly and on a heart level. To discuss feelings. Tim and I even have a joke that he "thinks," I "feel." And there may be more truth to that than I want to admit. But men can learn to talk, too. Wives can help. Ask questions. Probing, thoughtful, heart-sharing questions. Not "Yes" or "No" questions. There's not much conversation or sharing if you can answer yes or no and be finished. What are his hopes and dreams? What did he always wish he could do? If he won a million dollars, how would he spend it? What was his favorite toy as a child? Did she have a favorite teacher in school? What were her favorite classes? Who was his best friend growing up?

In the evening, don't just ask "How was your day?" Be creative. Ask something that requires more of an answer than "Fine" or "OK."

"What was the funniest thing that happened to you today? Who was the nicest to you at work? What was the toughest thing you had to do?"

Sylvia attempted to ask questions of her husband while out on a date. Conversation lagged. He wasn't a talker. So she asked, "What was the most interesting job you ever had?" She told us later, "I never heard him talk so much before. He talked and talked. I hardly got to say another word. I loved it!"

USE YOUR IMAGINATION. Like Sylvia, ask questions. Be creative. Ask serious questions. Silly questions.

"If stranded on a deserted island, what five things would you like to have?"

"If you could have dinner with anyone—living or dead—who would it be?"

"What is the most challenging [or fun] job you've ever had?"

"What's the worst thing you ever did as a child that you got [or didn't get] caught doing?"

"If you could change one thing about yourself, what would it be? Why?"

"What are the best three books you've ever read? Why are they your favorites?"

"When did you know without a shadow of a doubt that

you were committed to God?"

"What role does God play in your life? What difference has He made?"

Think up questions that will help you learn more about each other. That will inspire conversation. Sharing.

If you have a tough time coming up with questions or topics, check out the game Life Stories or a Serendipity Bible study. Many times you can find icebreaker questions that will open doors to conversation.

INCLUDE PRAISE AND THANKSGIVING. Praise your husband or wife. Say thank you, especially for things that too often go unnoticed.

He finally fixed the noise in that fan. She did the laundry. Again. When you appreciate something, say thank you. Tim brought my mom flowers one day when she came for dinner. I had e-mailed him to let him know that she was coming for dinner. I don't remember if it was a special occasion or not. It might have been when she got a promotion at work. But when he arrived home, he'd brought flowers for my mom. She was so surprised! So was I. After she left, he brought in a bouquet for me. "I couldn't bring another woman flowers without bringing them to you, too. But I wanted her to feel special, so I left yours in the car," he told me. I thanked him for bringing my mom flowers. It made me feel good that he cared that much about her. (I think I enjoyed her getting flowers more than getting them myself.)

Praise him for a good job. A great talent. Thank him for helping. For loving you. Praise her for being such a great mom to your kids. Let her know you think she's the best. I've read that we can perform "heart" surgery by the words we use. That it takes 40 good, positive comments to counter every negative one. For every one critical or demeaning comment we hear, we need to hear 40 positive, thankful, praiseful words.

We remember the negative so easily. Sometimes Tim tells me that I only remember the negative things he says. That I don't remember the good things. Attempt to remember the positive comments. Write them down. Each day I begin my quiet time with praise by keeping a praise journal. I write in it things I'm thankful for from the previous day. That's one way I remember the things Tim has done and said that I've appreciated. Once as a gift to Tim I made a plaque and listed many of the qualities I admire about him and the things I'm thankful for about him. We hung it in our bedroom so he could be reminded every day.

Some people believe that criticism and negative comments will inspire a person to try harder. They point out the bad instead of the good, believing that pointing out the faults will help the person improve. Try the opposite approach. Point out the good. Compliment the positive. I believe that encouraging words do more to inspire our future behavior than criticism ever does. I know I'm more likely to try harder or to do it again if someone compliments or appreciates what I've done. But when someone criticizes or complains about what I've done, I usually feel deficient in that area no matter how hard I try. And I attempt to avoid trying again. Or take a dislike to it.

Plus, when people constantly criticize us—even in an attempt to "help"—we tend to avoid them. Or feel that we just can't please them.

WEIGH YOUR WORDS CAREFULLY. Don't just fly off the handle. When confronting your spouse or telling him something he doesn't want to hear, think before you speak. Think through how to tell him that his actions or words impacted you in a hurtful way. Be able to explain why her words or actions made you angry. Choose your words carefully, for words do hurt. And in every relationship there are boundaries that you should never, ever cross; words that can cause pain for years to come.

What kinds of things? Personal attacks. Flinging a previous, bad mistake into your spouse's face.

By carefully wording what you want to say, you will avoid a lot of hurt. Instead of saying "You always . . . ," which puts a person on the defensive, try "I feel . . . when you . . ." ("I feel like a stupid little kid when you tease me for burning the potatoes").

It can make a difference.

"I found that when Ben and I would argue," Sarah told her friend, "he'd get furious and explode and walk away. I'd be left crying, wondering what in the world happened. I was only trying to get him to understand how I felt. Then I started watching what I was saying. Instead of saying 'You always try to tell me how to do things differently,' I said what I really meant. Something I'd never actually explained before.

"'I feel as though I can't do anything right when you tell me that I should be doing it this way or that way,' I told him. I was surprised at the difference! This was an area on which we'd been battling forever. But when I told him how I felt, he didn't get angry or walk away as he sometimes does. He said, 'I never meant to make you feel like you couldn't do anything. I just wanted to help you find an easier way to do it. I just wanted to help.' Then we were able to talk about how we could both handle it differently. It made a huge improvement."

Beginning sentences with "you always" or "you never"

causes a person to feel attacked. By changing the sentence to "I feel," you've switched the focus to you—not what the other person is doing wrong. It enables the person to understand—by sharing the feeling—and listen better, by not feeling attacked and on the defensive.

BE AWARE OF HOW YOU TALK ABOUT YOUR SPOUSE TO OTHERS. While this is not communication with your husband or wife, it still affects them. And it affects how others view your spouse, for better or worse. Sometimes what you say causes others to think less of your mate. You may not even realize what you're doing. I've done it. Too many times.

My granny can't understand why I won't let the stray kitties in the house. "Tim doesn't want cats in the house," she says, and it's the truth. He doesn't. And I'd probably end up letting them in despite the fact that they scratch up furniture and shed all over the place. But, you see, I've inadvertently let Tim take the blame for something that we both actually agree on.

I've overheard Granny telling friends that Tim doesn't like cats and won't let them in the house. You have to understand that my granny loves cats. She has cat things and figurines all over her home, and has two strays living with her right now. So she's not too happy with Tim. She's afraid the cats will get killed by the cars on the road, or too cold or wet or whatever. Instead of saying "Tim doesn't want the cats inside," I could have said, "*We* don't want the cats inside. They're strays, and they're not comfortable inside, either. They're very skittish. So we feed them outside."

Then Tim's not the bad guy. At least he's not the bad guy alone; it's both of us. (And despite what Tim may say, he does like cats. They greet him every evening when he arrives home, and he always stops to pet them and talk to them.)

That's a small example. But it shows how innocently and easily you can unknowingly cause others to think less of your spouse. Your friends invite you out and you say, "Sorry; my husband doesn't want me to go." They hear *Her husband tells her what she can and can't do.* Instead you could say, "That's not going to fit in my schedule this week," or "I'm sorry. I just can't make it. Let me know when you're going out again."

My mom wonders why I don't buy the canopy swing that I want for the yard. "Tim doesn't want me to spend the money," I tell her. She grumbles, "Tim never lets her have what she wants." (Not true.) I could have said, "I'd like the swing someday, but we don't have the money in our budget right now."

Thanks to a good friend, God continues to convict me of my need to be careful of what I say about Tim, and whom I complain to him about. Sometimes it does help us to vent with someone. But be careful whom you talk to. Complain to God. He'll still love your wife. Confide your complaints to others very carefully. At times I share struggles I have about or with Tim with my prayer partner, Sue. She knows how much I love my husband. She knows that when I complain, I'm not putting him down. I still love him. And she knows him well enough to know that he's not an ogre. That he loves me so very much. Often she'll remind me of this. She'll point out his good qualities. She sticks up for him and prays for us. And doesn't think less of either of us. She understands about marriage. That it's not perfect every day.

The people I try to be the most careful around when I talk about Tim are my boys. What I say about their dad will affect what they think about him. Whether it's when I'm talking about him to a friend and they're nearby playing *and listening* or when they're in the house listening to us talk, disagree, or me fume. Then sometimes they get mad at their dad and don't understand why he won't let them have a minibike or makes them work. How I respond to what they're saying then can influence what they're thinking about their dad.

Be careful not to vent your angry feelings or hurts when your kids are listening. Don't put your spouse down to your children or within their hearing. Even if your spouse isn't treating you right or your kids right, you don't have to say anything. The kids know. But in time they'll be angry with you because you put down their parent.

Vicki's marriage ended several years ago when her husband left her and the boys for another woman. He hasn't been very helpful or a part of their lives in the years since. But one of the things that I admire about Vicki is that she doesn't speak negatively about her ex-husband to the boys. He's their dad. She wants them to have a good relationship with him and does all she can to encourage that.

When our boys start harping about their dad—he won't let them do this or have that or makes them work—I point out how his actions show his love. I remind them of how much he loves them and that he's doing the best he can to take care of them. That he's doing what he thinks best. I admit that he's not perfect, but he loves them deeply. I pray that by reminding them constantly of his love, they'll understand. I know it can't take away their hurt and disappointment always. And sometimes I may not even agree with Tim. But I don't disagree with him in front of the kids. I go to Tim and talk to him about it. Many times I've tried to help him understand their viewpoint. Sometimes he changes his mind. But the kids don't know that I played a part in it.

How you talk about your spouse affects more than you

think. Be careful what you say and whom you say it to. And who's listening. Remember that kids tend to hear more than we think. And they understand much more than we give them credit for. Remind them of how much their father loves them. Point out how their mom shows that love. Be a cheerleader for your spouse.

Communication can help us to get to know each other better. It helps us to stay connected to each other. Without it, we'll be two strangers drifting apart. But sometimes communication is tougher than just trying to think about what we're going to say over dinner. Sometimes it means working through difficult moments in our marriages. Moments when we disagree. Even fight or argue. Moments that we'd rather not live through. We want it to be happily ever after, and the disagreements and hurts catch us off guard. Sometimes they scare us and cause walls to come between us. We have to talk through them.

I've already shared several things that have helped Tim and me as we've learned to work through problems. But I've learned the power of several other things that help in the heat of the moment.

PRAY. Pray as you talk. Pray silently. Pray together if you're both willing. It's hard to pray together and not work things through. Pray through your anger. Give God your feelings and expectations.

USE YOUR WORDS CAREFULLY. This is the time to say "I feel . . . when you" statements instead of casting blame with "You always" or "You never."

SHARE HONESTLY AND OPENLY. This was one of the hardest for me in the beginning of our life together. I've always been a people pleaser. I wanted to do or be whatever made everyone else happy. Trouble was, I couldn't make everyone else happy, and I was miserable. That's how I came into marriage. I wanted to please Tim. To say the things he wanted to hear. I didn't want to cause conflict or make him mad. I was afraid of telling him what I was really thinking and feeling.

In 1990 Tim had an accident that shattered both of his wrists. For the next six months he was home, and in the beginning he needed a lot of care. However, slowly and with a lot of determination he became more independent. A lot of things happened as the weeks turned into months. It was definitely a growing time for us. It was during the months of rehabilitation that Tim and I began really talking. I learned to tell him what I was truly thinking and feeling. Sometimes it made him mad. Sometimes it didn't, and the problem was a lot easier to solve than I had thought. And I learned to share more honestly. I learned that when I didn't tell him what I was really thinking and feeling, he would go away thinking that everything was OK when it wasn't. I was still hurting. Or upset. I just didn't show it. Constantly stuffing those feelings, keeping them to myself, caused me to feel unhappy in our marriage. At times I felt resentful and angry. Yet I kept it all bottled up. I think that because I did this, it made me an easy target for Satan. He could easily play on my unhappy feelings and tempt me to consider leaving.

Unless you're sharing honestly and openly, you're lying. You're really not working through the problems; you're just creating a temporary, surface peace. Underneath, things aren't peaceful. Your hurt and anger boils, and you're even more angry when you see how innocently happy your spouse is. *He* thinks that everything is OK. That the problem is solved. But you know it's not! It's not fair to him or to you.

It can be difficult to talk honestly and openly, and doing so can cause arguments. Tears. But all these things are necessary to reach true peace and happiness. True understanding.

But when you make the decision to share honestly, be aware of what you're saying. Think ahead, and have a few ground rules.

No storming out of the room. Plan ahead how to handle your anger if you get that angry.

Don't end the conversation until both of you are satisfied with the outcome. Don't give up on your marriage, no matter how long it takes. Marriage is for a lifetime.

Focus on the problem at hand—no dredging up past offenses or battles. Stick to the point in question.

Be careful how you talk. I can become very sarcastic. That's not allowed.

Let one person talk and share their point of view without interruption, and then let the other respond. Interruptions can blur what's being said and cause people to forget what they need to say.

Remind yourselves that you love each other. That you're not on opposite sides. You're not enemies. Remember that Satan is the real enemy, and he wants nothing more than for your family to be destroyed. What you and your spouse want is to reach the best solution for your marriage.

Make up. When it's all over, make the making up fun. Whether it's holding each other, kissing, or sharing a dish of ice cream, celebrate that you've made it to the other side. Celebrate your love for each other.

Great marriages don't just happen. They take time and effort and talk. Sometimes fun talk. Sometimes difficult talk. Sometimes deep and meaningful talk. But talk that draws you ever closer to each other.

CHAPTER 8

What Does God Think?

When we think of weddings, we think white lace and satin. Sequins and seed pearls. A church. Bridesmaids gliding down the aisle in long flowing dresses, carrying fragrant flowers. The majestic strains of classical organ music filling the church sanctuary and flooding into the foyer and out the doors. Men dressed in black suits with white shirts, looking uncomfortable and hot. Little kids dressed adorably while nervous parents wonder if they'll make it down the aisle without crying or dropping anything. Weddings always make me cry.

Just last week Tim and I attended a not-so-traditional wedding. The bride was beautiful in a beautiful ivory gown trimmed in lace and sequins. The men were in black and white. And the music was the traditional wedding music. But only those few things were familiar. Everything else was different. First of all, the wedding was held in a barn, an actual working barn. On the bride's grandmother's goat farm. They'd put in a new floor and stacked hay bails in a C shape at the front so that they formed the backdrop of the wedding. Guests sat in folding chairs next to walls of hay. The chairs on the aisles were decorated with lassos and bows.

The groomsmen were in black and white—black jeans, white shirts, black vests, black cowboy boots, and black cowboy hats. Their boutonnieres were little lassos with flowers. The groom was dressed similarly, only with a black waist-length jacket. Even the bride's father (my uncle) wore jeans, a vest, and a cowboy hat.

The bridesmaids wore long floral dresses and cowboy boots. Instead of lace or flowers their heads were crowned with cowboy hats dyed to match their gowns, and netting bows in the back. The bride wore white cowboy boots and a white cowboy hat.

Not a very traditional wedding. None of us had been to a wedding quite like it. Yet it was beautiful. The father of the bride looked dazed, the groom looked stunned, the bride looked radiant. And I cried.

The first wedding ever performed wasn't so traditional either. Eve wasn't in white lace and satin and Adam didn't wear a tux. There were no bridesmaids or groomsmen. No church. We don't even know if there was music, though there might have been an angelic choir.

God planned and performed the first wedding. He saw that Adam was alone. It was the first time God said that something wasn't good. As He had created the earth and all the things He filled it with, with each creation He had said "It is good." But being alone wasn't good for Adam (Gen. 2:18). He needed someone by his side. But in all of God's creation, there wasn't anything that God felt could meet this need (verse 20). No other creature would complement Adam's personality.

So God created Eve. He didn't create her from the dust of the ground as He had Adam. Instead He took a rib from Adam. He wanted to show that Eve was a part of Adam. I'm glad that He chose a part that was close to Adam's heart, protected under his arm, by his side. I think that's significant. I believe that it reflects what God desires in our marriage relationship. He wants man and woman to walk together, side by side. He desires for men to protect their wives and cherish them. The Bible tells us that "a man shall leave his father and mother, and be joined to his wife, and they shall become one flesh" (verse 24). One flesh. One person. Not one dominating the other. Not either losing their own individuality. But two people, blending their lives, loving the other as much as they love their own life.

God loves marriage. He created it. He said it wasn't good for man to be alone. He needed a wife. A helper. A companion. Someone to share life with. The good and the bad.

Jesus performed His first miracle at a wedding at which He and His disciples were invited guests (John 2:2). They weren't invited because of what Jesus could do for the wedding party. He hadn't performed a single miracle yet. They were invited because Jesus was a friend. The family wanted Him there, and He made a point to attend.

When they ran out of wine, His mother, also a guest, let her Son know the embarrassing problem. Scripture doesn't even say that she asked Him to do something. She knew her Son. She knew that whenever He saw a need, He took care of it. So she gave the need to Him.

"It's not time yet," Jesus told her, but that didn't deter her.

"Do whatever He tells you," she told the servants. And Jesus did tell them what to do. In the end the guests were served the best wine that they'd had throughout the several-day wedding. The bride and groom didn't even know that a miracle had been performed, that Jesus had impacted their wedding celebration.

Why did Jesus do it? Why was His first miracle turning water into wine? Why not something dramatic, as giving sight to the blind or raising the dead? Something that changed lives?

We don't know why. But I believe that it shows how much Jesus valued weddings. Marriages. He felt they were important enough to attend and important enough to use His divine power to remedy a social problem.

Both God and Jesus give their blessing on marriages. They value marriage.

The Bible often speaks of marriage. Giving commands. A wife is to be submissive to her husband, the way she submits to God (Eph. 5:22). A husband is to love his wife the same way Christ loves the church. That's a tall order, for Christ lay down His life for His people. He put His love for His people and their needs above His own life.

It shows the effect marriage can have on a person. First Peter 3:1 tells us that husbands can be won to the Lord by the witness of their wife. Not by the words they say, but by the way they live their lives, loving their husbands and God. Verse 7 tells husbands that they need to honor their wives and treat them with understanding so that their own prayer won't be hindered.

What does God think of marriage?

He esteems it. Created it. Saw the need for it.

He commands husbands and wives to love each other. To be submissive to one another. To treat each other with the same love and respect that He has for the church—for His people. What is His love like?

It's a selfless love, for Christ didn't think of Himself or

His comfort. He didn't consider what was easiest for Him. Christ couldn't imagine heaven without us. He didn't want to live in heaven if we couldn't be there. And so He left the glory of heaven behind in order to meet our great need for salvation. Living on earth, He taught the timeless themes of salvation in the words of the common people, telling parables of everyday life to help them understand God's love and grace. He understood their culture and thought processes, and how they scrambled to make a living on a little piece of ground or in their crowded, dirty towns. He spoke in ways that made God's love—which is so high and deep that it is beyond true comprehension—understandable to the simple men and women who gathered close to listen. He made God's love attainable. He met the needs of others before He met His own. Yet He made time alone with God a priority too. He never let His connection with His Father get lost among life's demands, or in the host of people who needed Him.

God wants us to love each other in the same way. Putting the other person first. Thinking of them. Their needs. Their desires. What is best for them. He longs for us to love each other so deeply that we can't imagine life without the other. He wants our hearts to be so close that nothing else is more important, except our relationship with Him. Through Christ, God gave married couples an example in communication: use words the other can understand. What does he know best? What does she like most? Use word pictures your spouse will understand. Take time to learn his love language, and use it. God wants you to understand your mate, and to be understood.

Sometimes we get hung up on the words "submissive" and "obey." Most brides prefer to promise "to love, honor, and *cherish*" rather than "to love, honor, and obey." We don't want people telling us what to do. And surely, neither husband nor wife should demand obedience of the other. We don't want people taking advantage of us. That's not what God had in mind either.

Yet God desires for you and me to obey Him, but not so He can randomly tell you what to do. Not a single one of His commands was made just for the fun of it. His commands provide protection from the evil Satan would do to us. God created us; He knows what we need, what our bodies need. What will enable us to live the most fulfilling lives. And so He gave commands to guide us and protect us as we live on this sinful earth. We're to be submissive to Him, but not so He can walk all over us and make us do things we don't want to do. God desires the best for us. It is His joy to crown our everyday lives with unspeakable joy and peace that is beyond understanding.

His desire—His command—for us to live submissively with one another is for the same purpose. We are to submit our will and our selfishness, and to think of the other person. If we love as He does, we will never be bossy or authoritative. We will love with a love that desires the best for our mate. We will put them and their needs above our own, helping them to live life to their fullest potential.

Think about this. If you both esteem the other more than you do yourself, then you both are affirmed. You both are lifted up.

How can we help our spouses reach their fullest potential?

First, you have to know them—their cares and struggles, their hopes and dreams. Their gifts and abilities. It's recorded in Genesis that God said that man and woman are to become one flesh. God wants a married couple to know each other more intimately than they do any other person on earth. That doesn't mean just physically. It's God's plan that we know each other intimately in all areas—emotionally, mentally, spiritually. In other words, that we become one flesh.

How well do you really know your spouse? What does he hope he can accomplish in his life? What are her dreams? Where is he spiritually? What is her biggest struggle? his greatest challenge? What are her strengths? his weaknesses?

We get to know each other by spending time together. Talking. Dreaming. Sharing. That's what this book has been all about. Taking the time to really get to know each other. To be there for one another.

As you know more and more about each other—always growing and learning more—then you can encourage and enable each other to reach your full potential

One way to do this is to dream dreams for the other person. In my book *The Gift of Friendship* I talk about dreaming dreams for your friends. It's equally if not more important to dream dreams for your spouse. Encourage them to dream, and to dare to strive toward the dream.

Tim has encouraged me in my writing every step of the way. He knows that from the time I was a little girl I've always dreamed of writing. It's the one thing I always wanted to do; even when I changed my mind about what else I would become—nurse, physical therapist, human and public relations specialist—I always wanted to write.

How has he dreamed this dream for me?

He bought me a computer. Encouraged me not to go back to work when the boys went to school, but to stay home for as long as I could and write. He made a copy of the first check I received for writing. Brought home flowers and ice-cream sandwiches the day I learned that *A*

Woman of Worth was number five for the publisher. He gives me time to write. Asks how it's going. Tells me not to rush, even if I have a deadline to meet.

Right now I'm dreaming a dream for Tim. He's got a beautiful voice and an incredible love for music. He uses those gifts to lead our praise and testimony time at church. But he would love to be a part of a quartet. Quartet music is his favorite. We wake up to The Cathedrals. We listen to them as we drive in the car. Hear them loudly singing on Sabbath mornings while we get ready for church. I bought him the biography of the lead singers.

I tell him that I'm dreaming of a quartet for him. I remind him often of what a great voice he has. I encourage him that he's doing a great job with the praise time and repeat the compliments people give me for him when they hear him sing or lead. And I'm praying. Praying that God will bring him a quartet. One day Zack found an ad for a quartet who needed a tenor singer, so we cut it out and taped it to the table where Tim sits. We thought it might be the answer, but Tim doesn't think that tenor is his part. I don't know that God will bring Tim into a quartet, but I know he has the gift and talent and enthusiasm for it. I dream and pray and trust God.

David wanted to be a paramedic. Or an emergency room nurse. He loved volunteering with the local ambulance company. Trouble was, he didn't have any training in the medical field. He was an accountant. Becoming a nurse would require going back to school, and *that* would require money and time. David had a family to consider— a wife and two kids.

Sherrie could have done the reasonable thing and said, "That's a nice ambition, David, but right now it's more important to pay the bills. Being an accountant isn't so bad." But Sherrie caught vision of David's dream and dreamed it with him. She increased her hours at work from part-time to full-time. Helped him fill out all the forms for school and prayed that he'd be accepted. Once he was in school, she helped him with his homework. Quizzed him while they did housework together. Took the kids out so he could study in peace. And encouraged him every step of the way, even when he wondered if he had made a mistake.

"I've never regretted those years," explains Sherrie. "It was tough. Money was tight. We didn't get a lot of time together. I was tired. He was tired. But it was worth it."

"I couldn't have done it without her," David adds. "Many times I wondered what in the world I'd done, giving up the security of my job to go back and start all over again. But I love what I'm doing. I look forward to going to work. I couldn't say that before. Accounting was just a job. This isn't. I can't believe Sherrie loved me that much to sacrifice so incredibly."

Dreams can be big or small. Fun or serious. But caring about the dream, encouraging it, giving it wings, and causing it to soar shows love. God's kind of love. For God dreams dreams for us too.

Accountability is another way of helping each other reach their full potential. We don't have a lot of accountability today. But it's needed. In all areas of our lives. We can hold each other accountable to being good stewards— of our time, money, resources. Making sure that we're taking the time for what's really important, such as spending time together without the children. Reminding him to call his parents. Taking time to play and relax.

Because we know each other so intimately, we can hold each other accountable in areas that others can't. Such as finances and integrity. Such as spending time with God.

And one of the most important ways we can help the other reach their fullest potential is to pray.

First, pray for one another. Pray deeply. Pray for more than just a blessing on his day or for her protection while she's driving. Really pray. Specifically. What are the needs on his heart? What would she like for you to pray for? If you don't know, ask. Say, "I'm praying for you. Is there anything particular I can pray about?"

Pray for his job. Ask her what her needs are at work. Is his job stressful? Does she have a lot of demands put on her each day? Is he witnessing to anyone? Pray for that relationship and the people involved. Pray for opportunities to witness at work.

Pray for him as a parent. Are there specific needs? Struggles?

Pray for her friendships. That God will give her godly friends. For mentors. That he will have strong friendships.

Pray for the struggles he faces in his life. The difficult relationships. Pray for her dreams and hopes. Pray for his integrity. Pray that the fruits of the Spirit will be evident in her life. Pray Scripture, claiming promises—especially in areas your spouse struggles the most.

I recommend a couple resources that can guide you in praying for your spouse. Stormie Omartian's *The Power of a Praying Wife* and a series that includes *Praying God's Will for My Husband* and *Praying God's Will for My Wife*. Both teach us to pray specifically, past the surface—deep, heartfelt prayers.

Second, pray together. Most couples aren't praying together unless it's the standard, "Lord, bless this food and the hands that prepared it." But hearing someone pray specifically for you, for your children, and for the things that are important to you is very meaningful and encouraging. It's something most wives I've talked to long for.

Tim and I haven't prayed regularly together, but I remember the times we've attempted to. I remember hearing him pray about things that I didn't know he knew or cared about. What an encouragement it was to hear him thanking God for me and for specific things about me. Usually when one of us is going to speak in public, the other will gather the boys around and the three of us will pray for that person. It means a lot. It reminds you that you have people on your side.

I believe that praying for one another and praying regularly together are the most strengthening things you can do for your marriage. Give it a try and see if my theory is right.

God created marriage. He blessed it. God commands us to love one another by being submissive to each other and loving with His kind of love. We can dream dreams and help each other become all that God intended. But what does God think of romance?

Turn to Song of Solomon, and you will discover a man and a woman who are deeply in love with each other. You'll find sheer romance. Listen to how they talk about each other. You'll probably want to use a modern translation or paraphrase, for it's a bit strange to think of your hair compared to a flock of goats (S. of Sol. 4:1). But in the beautiful, poetic language the Song was written in, such imagery was breathtaking. Imagine your husband saying, "You have ravished my heart with a glance of your eyes" (S. of Sol. 4:9, NRSV). Or what if your wife said "Kiss me! For your love is better than wine" (S. of Sol. 1:2, NRSV)? Take time to read this aloud just to yourself (or to each other). Hear the rhythm of the poetry as the Shulamite and her beloved talk to each other with word pictures that involve all the senses.

> "How beautiful you are, my love,
> how very beautiful!
> Your eyes are doves behind your veil"
> (S. of Sol. 4:1, NRSV).
> "I gather myrrh with my spice,
> I eat my honeycomb with my honey . . . .
> Listen! my beloved is knocking"
> (S. of Sol. 5:1, 2, NRSV).

These brief lines include the senses of sight, smell, taste, and hearing. Read on through this unique book and see if you can find the sense of touch, also.

No one reading this book could doubt that God wants married couples to have romance in their relationship. Passion. Fun. He longs for you to enjoy each other, to find the kind of pure delight in one another that you read about in the Song of Solomon. He created man and wife to belong together, to complete one another so that their love and happiness is an example of His love on this earth.

God created marriage. We need to take care of it as one of His precious gifts.

CHAPTER 9

Deadlines, Ratty Bathrobes, and Crying Children

Deadlines, ratty bathrobes, and weary, crying children are an inevitable part of real life. If your life is like mine, your days become so busy, so full of demands, that it's easy to let romance and intimacy slip away.

"Romance? What romance? Between work, the kids and our messy house, there's barely any time to talk, let alone be romantic," one tired wife sighs.

Cooking. Laundry. Driving the kids here and there. Helping with homework. Another church committee meeting. Yard work. Community service. How do you even think of romance in the reality of your hectic life?

When night comes, you're too tired to slip on sexy lingerie. You just want to crash and be comfortable. So you grab your ratty bathrobe and flannel pajamas—barely taking the time to brush your teeth, let alone comb your hair and splash on cologne. You fall into bed without thinking about how you look, much less wondering if you're attractive to your mate. You just want to sleep.

A couple decades ago a very unusual woman published a book about how to keep your husband happy. She said that when her husband came home from work, she greeted him in a different getup almost every day. Fantasy costumes. Saran wrap and little else. A fur coat and nothing else! He never knew what to expect when he came home. I don't know where she got all her ideas, or the energy. And where were the kids when Dad came home and Mom was wearing nothing but an apron and four-inch heels? Ooops, I guess they didn't have any.

Tim has seen me all different ways. Not because I planned creative ways to make him anticipate opening the front door in the evening. It's just part of life. He's seen me at my best—dressed to the nines and ready to go out. He's also seen me at my worst—baggy sweatpants, oversized T-shirts, and the raggedy blue sweatshirt I wear each morning when I go running. My hair uncombed, and grouchy. (Attitudes affect how we look, too.)

It works both ways. I've seen him dressed to the hilt in a tux for a friend's wedding. Wow! And I see him every evening when he gets home and gets comfortable. I've never seen such baggy sweatpants! Or ratty T-shirts. He heads out each morning for work looking very handsome. And I love seeing him up front at church in his dark suit and bright ties. I smile at the ornery twinkle in his eyes while he leads song service. He looks nothing like the guy working around our house all week, his hair sticking up every which way (like our son's hairstyle, but not quite so neat), and in grubby work clothes every evening. (If they pass the sniff test, they don't get tossed in the laundry.)

Ratty bathrobes and baggy sweat pants don't sound as

romantic as lacy lingerie, long, flowing dresses, and having every hair carefully tousled just right. But after working all day, we want to be comfortable at home. We want to be ourselves. We don't want to have to impress each other by dressing up. And that's OK. I even think Tim is kind of cute in his baggy, raggedy clothes. After he began working on the construction project, he didn't shave for a couple days. I liked the look and he's kept his beard looking like a couple days' growth ever since, much to my mom's dismay!

We don't have to dress up for each other all the time. Our spouses love us no matter how we look. However, how we look affects how we feel about ourselves. When I dress sloppy, I don't feel sexy or romantic. When I'm feeling heavy and ugly, I don't think of myself as very appealing to Tim. It helps *me* to feel better to dress up. For me, that's putting on a dress or a skirt. I love the summer when I wear lightweight dresses and sandals. They're as comfortable to me as shorts and a T-shirt, but in them I feel prettier. Sometimes I dress up for Tim, but most of the time I do it for me. Because I want to feel good about myself.

That's why I take the time to exercise almost every day. A quick walk around our country block. Some spot exercises such as crunches while I catch the morning news. I'm taking care of my body for *me*. Tim appreciates the benefits, of course, and I feel good when I know he enjoys how I look. But I take care of me for me so that I feel good about myself.

When I feel fat and ugly—and many times I do—I don't feel like being romantic. Romantic moments often lead to physical intimacies, and even though I know Tim loves me no matter what, when I feel ugly I don't feel sexy. I don't like for him to see my body out of shape. But even more than wanting romance or feeling sexy, exercising and taking care of my body gives me more confidence and energy. It's important to me, so I make it a priority. I get up earlier so I have time to fit it in. I combine it with other things I want to do, such as watching the news. And often I pray or plan while I'm walking. (I've written a lot of pages and practiced a lot of talks in my head while moving my feet.) I take the stairs instead of the elevator when I'm out running errands. I do my best to eat healthfully.

Romance and fitness can be combined too. Tim and I have hiked some pretty good trails together—enjoying the time with each other as well as the workout and scenery. We've also taken up biking. We saw the purchase of mountain bikes as an investment in our family. Biking was something just he and I could do, or we could enjoy as a family. We've taken the bikes and explored the nearby village of Strasburg, stopping for ice cream at the old-fashioned store on town square. We've attempted tennis together, "attempted" being more accurate than "played." Some may consider roller skating old-fashioned, but I still enjoy holding his hand on a couples' skate in the darkened rink. Often on the weekends Tim joins me for my morning walks.

Taking care of your body can help you feel good about yourself. When you feel good about yourself, it helps make your relationship stronger. When you feel lousy about yourself, you're likely irritable and grouchy, and think that no one else wants to be around you. You may believe that your spouse doesn't find you attractive and is even embarrassed by you. If you don't like yourself, you can't imagine how anyone else could like you either.

We need to take care of ourselves for us. Not to get to just the right size or shape. Not so that people will look at us or be attracted to us. But to help us feel good about who we are. Our size doesn't matter. Our perception of ourselves does. You can be a size 3 and hate how you look. Or be a size 22 and feel great. How we look is only a small portion of who we are, but a part that affects how we perceive ourselves in a big way.

How you dress affects how you feel about yourself, too. I don't feel romantic in my sweats. I much prefer to wear dresses, skirts, and jumpers. But my friend Katie hates to be in dresses. Instead of making her feel more attractive, she feels silly in them. For her, jeans or her favorite pair of khakis do the trick. Either way, both of us take the time to dress in ways that make us feel better about how we look.

I still wear my ratty bathrobe, and I often run around the house in the leggings and oversized T-shirts I put on for my walks. Tim thinks I look cute. He encourages me in my efforts to exercise. This week he bought me new running sneakers, for the ones I was wearing offered no support. The new sneakers are his way of taking care of me. Of showing me love.

But he appreciates that I take the time to dress nicely for him, too. He knows that I do it because I care. When I was growing up my dad often said, "Family is more important than company." Like most women, Mom wanted everything extra-special when company was coming over. But Dad thought the family was more important and deserved better than company did.

We may feel so comfortable with our mates that we can be ourselves and dress sloppy all the time, but making the effort to dress attractively shows that we care—about them and about ourselves. No matter how busy you are, at least once in a while you can take the time to look nice for your mate. Especially for those moments together. That date night, even if it's just going to the supermarket. Ratty bathrobes may be your daily routine, but wearing something lacy underneath once in a while adds a spark.

"I have two little girls, 2 years old and 6 months old," Nichole tells me. She is answering my question about romance while she cuts my hair. "My husband and I just went out together alone for the first time since the baby was born. We just don't have the time; the kids take so much time. And after working all day, I feel as though I need to be with them."

My own children, my two boys, are one of the greatest joys of my life. I smile whenever I think about them. I can't imagine not having them. But ever since they were born it's been hard to find alone time with Tim. Small children require so much attention. And when you're getting up several times a night with a crying baby, life feels a little foggy. At last they sleep through the night, but after a few months of relative peace they're walking, getting into everything, and talking nonstop. Then they're asking "Why?" 10 times an hour. You begin to wonder if you'll ever be able to think a complete thought again. Romance is a faded memory, surely not something that fits easily into your schedule.

Is it possible to have romance and children at the same time? Can you fit romance in between all your deadlines?

Yes, but not without a little effort.

One of the greatest challenges in spending a few hours alone together is finding the time to do it. Especially when children are involved, because our kids need our time too. And then there's everyone and everything else that demands your time. How do you squeeze in romance?

MAKE IT A PRIORITY. Let other things go in order to be

together. Set aside regular time to catch up, to talk, to snuggle.

"I put the girls to bed at 8:30. I know that a lot of their friends get to stay up later. But they need sleep, and I need that quiet time," shares Nancy, who has three little girls, 4, 7, and 9. "At least once or twice a week Roger and I spend that time together, talking, snuggling, whatever. There are a lot of things we could be doing instead. It's amazing how much I can get done without interruptions. But our marriage is important. We *make* the time. We'll never find it."

MAKE EVERYDAY MOMENTS ROMANTIC. When we're young and in love with being in love, our ideas of romance are different. Candles. Flowers. Sexy lingerie. As we grow and mature, our love does too. Things we never thought could be romantic are. Ordinary, everyday moments become special. Moments when we're working, playing, relaxing, talking on the phone.

One of the best "vacations" Tim and I had together was a working one. I was invited to speak at a retreat in the West. Since it was close to our fifteenth wedding anniversary we decided to make the trip together. A friend watched the boys for the long weekend. It was Tim's first flight. The organization that brought me out lent us a car and gave us directions to the camp, only a couple hours away. Happily we had an entire day to go those two hours, so they told us of a place to stop and hike. It was gorgeous! Breathtaking. I've never felt so close to God in nature as I did on that trail around a crystal-blue lake.

After I spoke in the mornings at the camp, we had the rest of the day to enjoy ourselves. We went horseback riding on mountain trails. Sailing. I watched Tim waterski and swim. At night the camp had moonlight boat cruises and a beach party complete with bonfires and S'mores. It was such fun. We felt so close. And it was good for Tim to see what I do when I'm away. (To be realistic, I must tell you that I don't usually have that much fun. This was truly a vacation trip.) Since then, any time life gets a bit stressful Tim says, "Are you ready to move to Idaho?" He's ready to go back because of the special times we shared.

The trip was more than just a moment—though it seemed all too brief—but romance doesn't need to take days. Minute romance renews you, too. Kissing your wife as she cuts veggies for supper. Coming up behind him and giving him a hug while he clears the table. Tim calling out from up on the scaffolding to tell me I'm pretty. Snuggling together for a few minutes in bed before rolling over to your sleeping positions. Connecting for a moment. Saying "I love you!" in a myriad of little ways.

SHOW YOUR LOVE BY HELPING YOUR MATE. "The other night I was running behind schedule. It had been a too-full day, and I was tired. After the kids were in bed I didn't feel like even looking in the kitchen, let alone doing the dishes. So I let them sit in the sink and planned on doing them in the morning. Harry and I relaxed for a little bit together. Just talking about what was happening in our lives." Linda has four children and an active household. "When I awoke the next morning the first thing I thought of was those dishes. But when I went to do them, they were done. Harry had washed them while I put the kids to bed, and hadn't said a word. I felt so cared for! It may be crazy, but it made me feel so very close to him."

Tim and I were talking about people we saw on the beach and about what made us attracted to someone. There were a lot of muscular guys walking around in bathing suits, and Tim thought I'd find *them* attractive. But he was wrong. "See that guy down there building the sand castle?" I told Tim. "He's been out there playing with his kids all afternoon. He's not muscular, and he's covered in sand. But I think he's one of the most attractive men on the beach. Not because of how he looks, but because he's out there playing with his kids. Laughing. Having fun. His wife is reading a book on a blanket a little bit down the beach."

Your mate's help speaks volumes of love, if you listen. His offer of takeout pizza when he found out what a tough day you've had. Or the time he takes to play with the kids. Or help around the house. She takes the time to clean the car inside and out because she knows that's how you like it, and it warms your heart.

One of the first events I planned for our conference women's ministries was for the day of prayer in March. It happened that our nearby academy planned a special day that Sabbath, so I planned vespers with a well-known prayer speaker for the end of the day. I was excited about it and put a lot into the planning. We'd have music and a special prayer time. And I just knew that everyone would come to hear the speaker. But the day was long, very long. People sat on metal folding chairs for hours. When the day's events were over, *I* was ready to go home. Yet I had to lead out in the vesper service I'd put so much time in planning.

Almost no one came. I wasn't surprised. I was disappointed, but I understood. And there was Tim. Taking the bulletins and having our boys help him hand them out to the people headed for their cars. Trying desperately to herd people into our meeting. It didn't bring in more people, but it did touch my heart. I knew that my husband loved me. He wanted so very much for this event to be a success for my sake. He didn't want me to be disappointed.

Tim was tired and probably just wanted to go home too. But he did his best to help me. The service was a blessing. The music, speaker, and prayer time was exactly what my heart needed. Less than a dozen of us attended, and somewhere in the hall was my husband, entertaining two little boys who just wanted to go home.

Tim has helped me all he can with my writing and ministry, even when he doesn't quite understand why I'm doing what I'm doing. To me, that speaks love.

INCLUDE THE KIDS IN ON THE DATE. We need to have time alone, just the two of us, on a regular basis. But sometimes we can squeeze in those intimate moments with the kids right there. Mary and Steve canoe in one canoe while the boys take the other. Josh and Zack helped me plan out everything when I kidnapped Tim for his birthday. While they climbed around the rocks on the Gettysburg battlefield, Tim and I strolled hand in hand, talking, enjoying watching the boys, taking in the quiet moments. We've lingered around the campfire for a few minutes after we've sent the boys to their sleeping bags.

"Mike and I have taken the girls to places that were special to us when we were dating." Stacy and Mike have two preschoolers. "Mike will say, 'This is where Mommy and I . . . ' and he'll tell them about our dates. The girls think it's neat. They like hearing stories about Mommy and Daddy. Then while they play, Mike and I reminisce. It may not sound romantic, but it makes us feel closer together."

In our busy, demanding lives the urgent often screams for our attention while what's truly important to us gets pushed to some other time. We need to make time for romance, but more important, we need to find romance in the midst of it all.

CHAPTER 10

Married to an Opposite

Tim and I went for a walk this morning. I'd gotten up early and finished all the things that I had to do. Lunches were packed. The house was straightened up. I love getting up early and having my quiet time with God, and being able to get a few things accomplished before having to face the day. When everything was done, I woke up Tim. It took a couple tries, but finally he stumbled out of bed and into his sweats, and we hit the road. I had to laugh to myself while we were walking. I was thinking about this chapter and realized how even going for a walk showed our differences. I was ready for the walk. Had gotten up early. Was walking fast, moving my arms, looking at everything, talking to Tim every step of the way. Tim had stumbled out of bed and into his sweats. He walked silently with his hands in his pockets. I wasn't sure if he was awake or not.

Not only do Tim and I walk differently—

and get up in the morning differently—but we're opposites in many ways. The way we view life, approach problems, and make plans. We have different approaches to parenting, friendships, and watching TV (with Tim flipping from one station to another, never staying on one channel long enough to really tell what the program is about, but maybe that's a man thing).

I recently took the Myers-Briggs Type Indicator personality test (the MBTI). This test rates your preferences in four different areas: extraversion/introversion, sensing/intuition, thinking/feeling, and judging/perceiving. The test was fun to take, and the results didn't really surprise me.

While the facilitator was going over the results with me, explaining each different indicator, I attempted to figure out Tim's personality. I wasn't surprised that his preferences were the opposite of mine, for our personalities are so different.

Tim tends to be introverted. I'm an extrovert. He loves peace and stillness. I love being involved in everything that's going on. When he's faced with decisions or big jobs, he wants it quiet so he can think. (Too often he's trying to think and I'm chattering away.) I get energized by excitement, busyness, and a lot going on. I start talking faster, and moving faster—rushing around, doing a million things at once. My mind races as fast as I do. Tim, who likes to take things slow and quiet, gets overwhelmed and often tells me, "Slow down!"

Tim prefers "sensing." He tends to focus on the present and concrete information—what is actually happening. He's very practical. My indicator was "intuition" (though just slightly). I tend to look at the possibilities, thinking, *How could this be done better? What else could we do? What would make it more effective or better?* I look at the big picture, not just the facts. Tim often groans when he hears me say, "I have an idea!" In his mind there is a right way to do everything. And that's the way you do it.

While I tend to go on my feelings, Tim is a thinker. He bases his decisions on logic and after analyzing all the data. He'll check out *Consumer Reports* and shop for something in every store he possibly can. He wants to know every detail he can find out. And he doesn't like to make a decision till he's exhausted every possible source. I look at the data, but rely on my feelings. We've often said that he thinks and I feel. The test showed that there's a lot of truth to that.

Just this week we went shopping for carpet for our new upstairs addition. I was happy with the first store we went to, and thought that the color of the carpet I found was wonderful. The salesman was nice and seemed to know what he was talking about. The price was good, and they could install it the next week. After having our new addition under construction for more than a year, I was ready.

But Tim wanted to check out more stores. A week and several stores later, we finally went back to the first store and ordered the carpet I liked. Tim had to do all the research to make sure he was making the best decision. I would've just gone with the first store because I liked the color and the salesperson. For Tim the process of making the decision is important. He has to go step by step, checking out all the facts. He can logically show how he comes to a decision. I can't always explain how or why I've made a decision. Funny, though, we often come to the same conclusion.

Because I am more feeling oriented, I tend to be very sensitive. My feelings often get in the way. Tim says I'm overly sensitive, and maybe he's right, for I read things that aren't there into comments he makes. Especially comments that I hear as critical, even though Tim may simply be trying to help me. Sometimes he tells me something and expects me to say "Oh, thank you, honey." But what I've heard is "You're not doing that good enough." What he's said makes me *feel* that he thinks I'm dumb or not doing something right. But usually that's not it at all. He's just trying to help me do a better job. He thinks he's helping and can't understand why I get so hurt.

I remember coming home one Sunday evening from a women's retreat to find him with the refrigerator and stove sitting in the middle of the kitchen floor. He was cleaning the floor under where they had both been sitting. He smiled and greeted more warmly. "I thought I'd help you out, hon," he said, but that's not what I was thinking. My thoughts started racing. *He doesn't think I clean the house well enough. He expects me to move these appliances out and clean under them every week!* Of course, that's not what he was saying. He was honestly just trying to be nice to me. I must constantly look for the reality in the situations and not just go on my feelings.

Tim and I both tend to be organized and like to have our work areas organized. We both want things in their places. But those places are different. Tim likes piles. *I* want things put away. What's organized to him isn't to me. At times it's funny, for he'll put something down where I don't think it belongs. I come by, see it there, and almost without thinking put it away. (I'm innocent. I don't realize that he's still using it.) I believe that everything has a place and that's where it needs to be. Pillows sit just so on the sofa. Pictures must hang straight. When my environment is out of order, I feel out of order.

While I like my space organized—whether it's our home or my desk at work—I'm not as particular about my schedule. I do plan out my schedule, organizing it, deciding what to do each day. But I tend to be very flexible. Something comes up, and I'll change without getting upset. I like variety. Tim likes routine. Sometimes I tease him that he could eat the same breakfast, wear the same outfit, eat the same lunch, and work the same hours for the rest of his life and be happy. I like wearing a different outfit everyday. If I tire of one job, I need to go on to something else. That's why I like jobs that allow me to vary what I have to do. Tim has worked at the same company for more than 20 years. He's attended the same church most of his life. And we'll probably live in our home until Jesus comes.

However, while I fill in my schedule months in advance (and fill it full), Tim hates to be scheduled in advance. He can't stand a full schedule. He likes to decide what he wants to do when he wants to. He can't remember what's on our calendar, though I can recite what's going on every weekend for months, the date, and what we'll be doing. He counts on me to remember and keep him on track. Normally I wait until it's right upon us before telling him. (It gives him less time to be unhappy about it.)

I'm more people-oriented. I love being with people. I feel deeply, and continually take people's feelings into consideration. When someone shares with me, my heart goes out to them. I want to cry with them, laugh with them. Many times I'm more upset over problems and conflicts between people than those involved. Tim stays fact-oriented. He can separate himself from the feelings and people involved and focus on the facts. He can make decisions based on the facts without worrying what people will think about the decision or how they'll feel about it.

We approach many decisions like that—me thinking about the people, him thinking about the facts. When we were talking about buying mountain bikes, Tim thought about the cost, what kind of bikes we'd buy, and how we would get them to where we would ride. I thought about how much fun it would be to be able to ride together as a family. I pictured riding along wooded paths, eating picnic lunches, and enjoying being together. He saw the bikes as a financial expense. I saw them as an investment in our family.

Neither Tim nor I are right or wrong. We're just different, and our differing personalities show up in big and small ways.

I cry at commercials. Tim just shakes his head and thinks about the product.

I take in every stray. He thinks of how much it's going to cost. (We've fed as many as eight stray cats at our back door at a time.)

He's a night person. I'm a morning person.

He'll eat anything. I have to recognize what I'm eating.

He likes vanilla ice cream. I want to try all the flavors.

He's quiet. I'm talkative.

He's focused; he deals with one thing at a time. I enjoy busyness, juggling several things at a time.

He saves every penny. I love buying gifts and new clothes, and going out to dinner.

Tim and I are opposites. Sometimes I wonder what God was thinking when He put us together. Why didn't He make us more alike? Why do so many people marry opposites?

Often our differing personalities attract us to each other. I was attracted to Tim's stability, his strong work ethic, and his reliability. I appreciated his ability to make decisions without letting feelings get in the way. He enjoyed my enthusiasm and creativeness, and the way I cared about others. My constant talking amused him. I think he liked my energy; I could get so much done in such a short period of time.

But often the very traits that have drawn a couple together irritate them. We like and admire traits that are different from our own, but in everyday living they can drive us crazy. I can get frustrated that Tim works over so many evenings. I want him to spend more time with me and the boys, just having fun. And when Tim's trying to focus on something, my talkativeness can get on his nerves. Often he wants me to slow down. And he gets frustrated with me when I'm busy doing lots of things and he's still attempting to decide what to do.

Wouldn't life be easier if we were both the same?

It might be easier, but it wouldn't be as fun. Imagine if both you and your husband were the same. If you were both quiet, it would be hard to have conversations. If you were both talkative, you'd be competing for "air time." If you were both workaholics, you'd spend all your time working and no time together. If both of you were feeling-oriented, chances are each would constantly be getting hurt by the other. When both partners see "possibilities," who rolls up their sleeves, gets in there, and gets things done? Or if you both are the kind that deals in the "now" and not in the "future," who would dream the dreams that keep life interesting and bring fulfillment?

Being married to opposites gives our lives balance. God created us to complement each other, to complete each other. Tim needs my love for people to help him understand how people feel and how his behavior or decisions could affect someone. I need his facts to help me make better decisions. We each compensate for the other's weaknesses.

But how do you and I survive the differences between us and our spouses?

Realize that being different doesn't mean being wrong. If your spouse isn't like you, it doesn't mean he's wrong—or that you are. It just means you're different. You approach life differently. He makes decisions differently. It's as if you are each a piece of the puzzle. And putting both pieces together makes the picture complete.

Realizing that being different isn't wrong is the first step in understanding your mate. Tim knows that I'll always be busy. He realizes that I like it that way. While he doesn't understand, because he'd much rather have things slow and quiet, he accepts that it's a part of who I am. We have to understand that we're different and accept it. Trying to change someone to make them like we think they should be usually doesn't work. It just frustrates.

Harold loves a crowd. He's the life of every party, talking, joking, making new friends. Harold has never met a stranger. His wife, Sophie, can't stand a crowd, and tends to shrink into the shadows at parties. She prefers working in her flower garden by herself to being with a crowd. The thought of spending hours on end by himself in a flower garden—or anywhere—drives Harold crazy. He loves people.

"When we were first married, I just couldn't understand why Sophie didn't just jump into conversations. I kept pushing her to be more friendly. I'd take her places and try to force her to be a part of everything that was going on," Harold says. But Sophie shrunk even further into the shadows. He had to learn that Sophie just didn't enjoy being around a lot of people. She preferred one-on-one conversations. Her friendships were few but strong. Friendships that lasted a long time. Harold realized that while he had a lot of friends, he didn't have deep friendships. He was learning the next step.

APPRECIATE THE DIFFERENCES. Respect your spouse's differences. It's what makes them the person you love. Harold realized that one of the things that had drawn him to Sophie was her quietness. "She always had this peace about her, and she could listen so intently. Most people listened, but they didn't really hear or care. Sophie listened and heard and understood. She wasn't like other people." On the other hand, Sophie loved to watch Harold talking to everyone. She admired his comfortableness with strangers. She admits she's often wished she could make people feel good about themselves the way he does.

ALLOW YOUR SPOUSE TO BE DIFFERENT. Don't try to change him or make her conform to what you think she should be. God created us uniquely. Individually. Not to be carbon copies of each other.

When Tim and I were first dating, he was bound and determined to change me. For my own good, of course. He thought he knew how I could change to be a better person. Back then, believe it or not, I was quiet. While I loved being around people, I was too shy most of the time to participate in conversation, and I definitely did not start one with someone I didn't know. I have piles of "love letters" he wrote to me, with a constant theme. Tim wanted me to be more outgoing and assertive. To stand up for myself more. And he kept pushing me to change. For my "own good."

Back then Tim didn't appreciate that I was just different from him. I felt shy around his friends. While they were all talking and laughing, usually about high school experiences that they'd had together but I hadn't been a part of, I just sat and listened. I'm not the type to laugh out loud a lot, either. They'd be having a great time reminiscing and laughing, and I'd just be sitting there quietly. (It's not because their stories weren't funny. They did some pretty crazy things.)

For a long time he tried to make me more like him. After a while he just quit trying. He began to accept me for who I was. (Later, as I grew in my relationship with God and found confidence and security in Him, I was able to let go of the fears that kept me shy, and now I'm much more outgoing. And as I've said, now sometimes Tim wishes I were a little less talkative.)

LEARN FROM YOUR SPOUSE'S DIFFERENCES. They often point out an area in our lives that needs some change. God gave us an opposite to teach us how to grow. Many times we were attracted because we saw a strength we didn't have but wanted. Allow God to use your spouse's strengths to help your weak areas to grow. Harold learned to take time to be quiet. He learned to spend time with just one person at a time, building lasting, strong friendships instead of always playing the crowd.

EXPECT PROBLEMS. We'd all love to live "happily ever after," but it doesn't happen. Conflicts will come. Our differences will get in the way. Not just our different personalities, but differences from the way we were raised, what we expect from life, and what we hope for the future.

Tim likes to put away money for the future. While I know that's important and I want to too, I don't always want to be as frugal as he is. I want to use some of our money to enjoy life now. That can cause conflict about how we may spend money or save it. We both had a couple different opinions about how we wanted to rear our children. One point of conflict grew around mealtimes. I grew up in a family that allowed us children to take only what food we wanted to eat (and liked), which means I rarely ate anything green. We never had to clean our plate if we tasted a food and didn't like it, or if we got too full. But Tim believed that a child should be given a little (and his "little" was always more than mine) of everything and made to eat it. It caused a lot of battles. I agreed that I wanted our kids to try everything—there were so many things I was unwilling to try as a kid—but I didn't want to force them to eat something they didn't like. (Too well I remembered gagging over certain foods.)

It took a while to work through the conflict. We tried Tim's way, making the boys sit at the table until their plates were clean, but I hated it. I didn't like mealtime being a battle. We worked through the conflict by compromising. The boys still had to try everything, but if they didn't like something and didn't want to eat it, they didn't have to. But if they didn't clean their plates, they had to wash the dishes. (Many times they were willing to finish something they didn't like so that they didn't have to do the dishes. And at times they gladly did the dishes in order not to have to eat something. Today it's not a problem.) Compromise is an important step in working through conflict.

COMPROMISE. Because I love being around people, I'd invite someone home after church for dinner every week if I could. While Tim doesn't mind company, he really enjoys quiet Sabbath afternoons. After a hectic, stressful week, he just wants to relax, not entertain. This difference used to cause us problems. Too many times I invited people home without checking with him first, only for him to be upset that his house was going to be full of people all afternoon instead of the quiet that he'd looked forward to. Yet I felt as if every time I asked if I could invite someone home, he said no. We talked about it and decided that we'd always check with each other before inviting Sabbath company, and that he would be willing to have people over more often. It's funny that the person who first broke this rule was Tim. He invited a family home after church one week without asking me first. It was fine with me once I got over the shock and started planning what I could serve for lunch.

Holidays and celebrations were another area in which we learned to compromise. In my childhood home, birthdays, Christmas, and Easter were big celebrations. Mom always made a big deal out of holidays. I remember birthday parties complete with balloons, streamers, and tiny paper cups of mints and peanuts by our plates. We'd play pin the tail on the donkey and other games before opening presents and eating cake. At Christmas our family had a huge Christmas dinner with grandparents and presents galore. At Easter, we awoke to Easter baskets at our places at the table. (I always got up early and sneaked down to "trade" the marshmallow chickies out of my basket for the chocolate in my brothers' baskets.) There'd be a big meal, with grandparents, aunts, uncles, and cousins, and of course, the traditional Easter egg hunt.

In Tim's family the holidays passed more quietly, and we still see the differences today. At my mom's, celebrations include the 10 cousins, my three brothers and their wives, my aunt and uncle and their three children and their spouses, Granny, Mom, and us. There's always a lot of noise and talking. Tim's family's gatherings are much simpler and quiet. Sometimes there's no one there but his parents and siblings, Grandmom, and us. People talk quietly, with usually only one conversation going on at a time. At my mom's there are three or four conversations going on at any given time.

You can guess the challenge Tim and I had when it came time to celebrate anything. Naturally I wanted to make a big deal of every holiday, and Tim couldn't understand why. He doesn't like a lot of fuss. Eventually we compromised. Our holiday and birthday celebrations don't have quite the hoopla I was used to, but we've begun our own traditions. When Tim turned 40 his friends were surprised that they didn't get invited to a party. I've given fortieth birthday parties for many of our friends, but I respect Tim and knew he wouldn't enjoy it. We had our own family celebration.

The boys and I blew up balloons and strung crepe paper in our kitchen. We bought a couple presents and made the meal and cake he requested. (That's one of our traditions—the birthday girl or guy gets to "order" the dinner and dessert that they want.) But no one else was there.

Instead of a lot of presents for Christmas (as I had, growing up) we give our boys three gifts each. And no clothes allowed, unless they request them. We choose gifts that they want. Tim prefers giving practical things, but I like to buy something a person wants but doesn't necessarily need. That makes it extra-special.

It takes a little working out, but as Tim and I sit down and talk about what is important to each of us, we learn how to compromise in a way that makes both of us happy. You can do that too.

Alicia and Chris compromise on vacations. He loves the quiet of the outdoors, so he wants to go backpacking and hiking. She'd rather mosey through the little tourist shops at the bottom of the mountain. So they compromise. They hike by day and shop in the evening. At night they stay in little inns and motels out of the high-traffic areas.

Compromise may mean stepping out of your comfort

zone every once in a while. It means that a "reclusive" spouse will go to a party and make a real effort to enjoy it for the benefit of the partner who loves to go out. Compromise happens when a husband who does only what's on his calendar or to-do list is occasionally willing to skip the list and do something "outrageous" with his spontaneous wife.

It may mean trying something new that you wouldn't normally try. As Tim and I have built the addition on to our home this past year, I've learned to do a lot of things that I never thought I would. Honestly, I never thought I'd need to. But it was important to Tim that I try. So now I know how to measure, cut, and hang drywall. I've laid a lot of the tile in the bathroom; even learned to measure and cut some of it. It would have been easier to stay downstairs while he worked, but I knew it was important to him that I help and share the experience.

Living with an opposite and not going crazy means taking the time to understand your mate. Understanding why they respond the way they do and how they look at life. It means accepting them for who they are *without trying to change them*. Knowing that just because they aren't the same as you, or see things the same way, they're not wrong. Just different. It takes effort learning to compromise and to be willing to try new things. But giving your partner the freedom to be himself or herself, letting yourself be challenged by his or her strengths, helps you to grow too.

Couples may be different in an infinite number of ways. Here are a few:.

Dependent and independent
Affectionate and reserved
Perfectionist or not

Pessimistic and optimistic
A spender or a saver
Serious and funny
Assertive/aggressive and shy

What is most important is that you have the same commitment to each other and to your marriage. That you have determined to love each other no matter what. To treat each other with respect even when we don't understand each other. And to allow God to work in your lives to change you—or not change you—for the better.

The Bible says that when a man and woman are married, they become one. But that can take a l-o-n-g time. However, as you combine your different outlooks and personalities you *do* become more like each other. You become a more whole one. And just as God pronounced at the end of each day of Creation, that's *good*.

CHAPTER 11

R-O-M-A-N-C-E

I really surprised her that time." Steve chuckles as he recalls the romantic anniversary surprise he planned for Tina. "We were headed to my family's home for the weekend. When we were a couple hours away I told her that I was getting tired and thought maybe we should stop for the night and finish the trip in the morning. She offered to drive since we were so close. I drove for a while longer, and when we got about an hour away I said, 'I just can't go any farther. We're going to have to stop for the night.' She wasn't too happy. We'd passed all the exits with cheaper hotels, and she didn't want to pay a lot for a hotel, especially since we were so close to where we were going. So we agreed that I'd run into the hotel to find out how much it cost, and if it was below a certain price, we'd stay. If not, she could finish driving. When I came out, I told her that it was under the cost and we headed to our room. She was surely surprised when she found flowers and a chilled bottle waiting for us, but I'd made the reservations in advance. Planned the whole thing. I'd known all along that we were going to stop before we got to Mom's, and have a romantic evening before heading into our family weekend."

"Phil didn't tell me where we were going, except that it would be out of the country and that he'd give me a two-hour notice when it was time to leave." Jan's husband had planned something special for their twentieth wedding anniversary. "The day we left we headed into Canada and spent a night at a nice hotel. We left the car there and got in the hotel shuttle for the airport, I thought. Phil even asked the guy how long it would take to get to the airport. After we dropped off a couple passengers, Phil told the guy that we had a little time and asked him to stop at the port. That's when he showed me the tickets. He had booked us on a cruise to Alaska! We spent the next week on the cruise ship, eating, relaxing, just seeing the incredible, beautiful scenery and sights. It was wonderful. I never dreamed that the surprise would be a cruise. When we got back we had to go to the hotel to pick up our car, and I told Phil I wanted to go into the hotel restroom before starting home. When I came out, Phil said, 'Let's check out the fourth floor first.' Once up there, he handed me the keys to the presidential suite. He had booked us one more night in luxury before heading home! We picked up takeout pizza and salad and ate it in the presidential suite while watching the Mariners game. I just couldn't believe it!"

Many times when we think of romance, we think it has to be made of incredible moments like these. Surprises. Getaways. Experiences to be remembered forever. Moments that just take your breath away. But romance isn't limited to well-planned-out, down-to-every-detail,

never-forget rendezvous. Romance can also be those simple moments. Spontaneous times. Opportunities that
sneak their way into our everyday lives.

In your busy life, with everything else you're juggling, the
incredible dates will be few and far between. Yet you still
need romance, still need special times when you and your
spouse feel close and loving. You must connect with each
other in order to still be a couple. So it's the romance in the
midst of the chaos and busyness that's most important.

A flower picked from the garden and left on her pillow.

An old-fashioned, mushy love letter, sprayed with perfume and sent to him at work.

Carving your initials in the ice on her car as you leave
for work, so she'll find it when she heads out. (This idea is
inspired by the friend who told me that when she was
younger, her boyfriend carved their initials into the ice on
every windshield on her block while doing his paper route.)

A phone call in the middle of the day just to say "I love
you!"

Baking his favorite dessert for supper.

Taking her shopping for something new to wear.
A dress. Pretty underthings.

Holding hands.

"This may sound silly, and probably isn't romantic."
Olivia hesitated before sharing her idea of a romantic
moment with her husband. "But for us, it's playing Frisbee.
Dan enjoys sports, and I don't. Frisbee was something we
could both do together. We've played frisbee at the shore,
in parks while the kids play nearby, and at church picnics.
Playing Frisbee gives us an opportunity to connect—just
the two of us. Something that's special for us. We've tossed
the Frisbee around since we were dating."

"Romance? Romantic moments? I'm not sure what

those are," laughs Wendy when I asked her what she and her husband did that was romantic. "With two little ones, we don't get much time to talk, let alone do anything together. But sometimes it's something as simple as sitting together watching Cory play. Just sharing those simple moments together helps us to reconnect in the midst of the chaos of our lives."

And that's what romance is all about. Connecting. Reconnecting. Continually building the relationship you have. Constantly learning about each other. Growing together. Because if we don't grow together, we'll grow apart.

What happens when we don't include romance in our lives?

"I start feeling grouchy and irritable when Fred and I haven't had any time together." Margaret and Fred have been married 18 years and have three teenagers. "It feels as though I'm having to deal with everything on my own."

"It's easy to forget about romance and spending time together," Charlie said. He worked two jobs while his wife worked full-time too. "Betty and I have been so busy just trying to keep up with work and the things around the house. Finding time to sit and talk or do something together is about impossible. Pretty soon we're strangers. I have no clue what's happening in her life—how her job's going or what she's thinking about. And she doesn't know what's going on with me, either.

Once it got so bad that I heard, through one of her friends, that she'd been having a really rough time at her job. Betty and I hadn't talked in so long. We both worked all day. We'd come home for supper and watch the news while we ate in silence. Then I'd head out for my part-time night job. By the time I fell into bed she was already asleep. Then one day at church her friend commented about how well Betty was handling such a difficult situation at work. That if it had been her, she would've quit. And I looked at Betty across the room and realized I had no clue what she was facing. I felt as though I'd abandoned her, and let me tell you, that was a turning point. We started keeping the TV off and talking during supper. I eventually quit my second job. We bought a used tent and started spending weekends camping together. Sure has made a difference!"

"I didn't even see it coming. Jon and I had been married for a number of years, and I was home full-time with babies. He was working two jobs. He'd come home from work tired and grouchy. Eat dinner in silence and head out for the second job. The guy next door started talking to me whenever we were both outside at the same time. He was just so nice. Low-key. But he'd compliment me on how I looked—I was trying to lose weight after the last baby— and was helpful with the yard work. Jon wasn't able to help with anything." Patty shares an especially difficult time in their marriage. "One day I realized that I was looking forward to seeing this guy. That I was making sure I was dressed nice and watching for him so I could 'accidentally' run into him, but I wasn't looking forward to Jon coming home. Jon was so tired and grouchy that all I looked forward to was his heading out again. At that, I knew we were in trouble. I started praying about it right away. It was amazing how God worked. The neighbor moved and I started looking for ways to make Jon's life easier, such as offering back rubs. I took care to look nice when he came home and began taking a nap now and then when the kids did, instead of using that time to get things done all the time. That way I wouldn't be too tired to wait up for Jon. He'd tell me about his day while he got ready for bed, and I'd tell him what went on in mine. We knew we loved each other. We just kind of lost sight of what was important."

When you and your husband don't spend time together, talking, caring, sharing, and showing love to each other, you're going to drift apart. You'll be more easily tempted to become involved with others—even if it's just emotional and never gets physical. You won't be able to be the support and strength to one another that God intends. Husbands and wives must be committed to spending the time it takes to be friends. To staying connected with each other. To become one flesh. The benefits will last a lifetime.

Romance is one way of showing love, of providing a place to grow closer. In the midst of all you have to do and need to do, romance happens when you take the time to stop and find each other. The following acronym reminds me what romance is all about.

R: REMEMBER THE SMALL DETAILS. Take time occasionally to create the mood—candles, music, environment.

O: OWN YOUR MARRIAGE. Don't let it coast. Take responsibility.

M: MAKE AN APPOINTMENT with your mate for an evening out or in. A day. A weekend. An hour. But spend time together. Write it on your calendar and guard that time.

A: ALWAYS SAY *I LOVE YOU.* With words and without. Find out how your mate "hears" love and speak his language. Let her know you love her every day in some way.

N: NEVER STOP PRAYING FOR YOUR SPOUSE. Prayer is the

rope that binds us together.

C: CREATE A STRESS-FREE ZONE. Whether it's the time you spend or a place you can go, don't allow stress or problems or interruptions in.

E: ENCOURAGE YOUR THOUGHTS TO WANDER TO YOUR MATE. Think about him. Let her know you're thinking about her.

As you include romance in the everyday, ordinary, already too-full, activities of your life, you will feel loved and become stronger. Your marriage will become the refuge that God desires it to be, the example of His love and care.

Marriage will be the place we learn who we are and dream to be all we can be. Together.